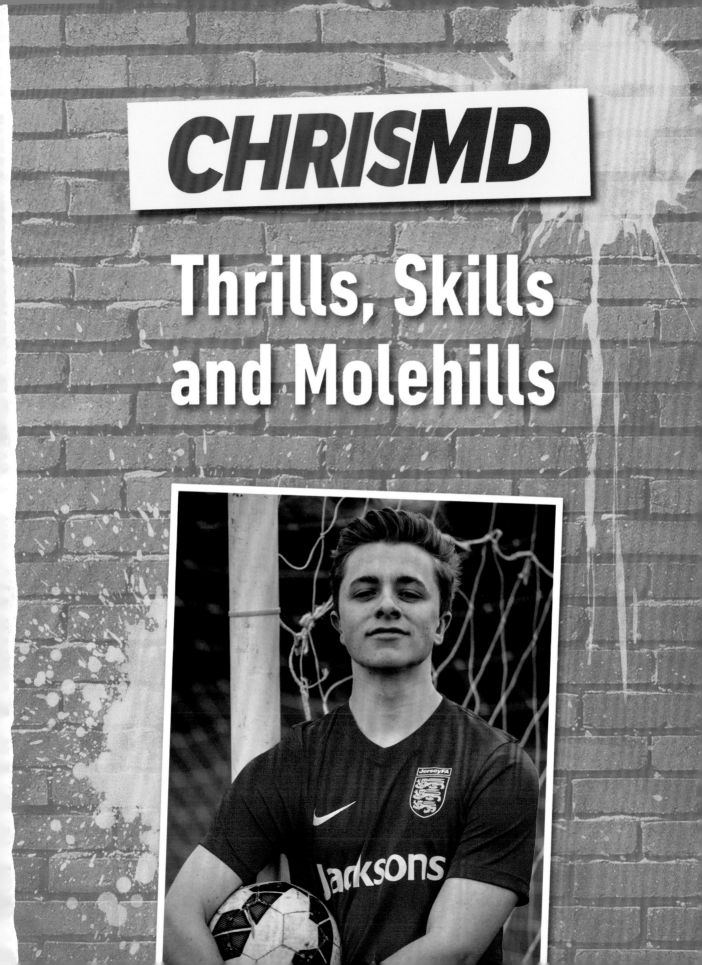

CHRISMD

Thrills, Skills and Molehills

PUFFIN BOOKS

UK | USA | Canada | Ireland | Australia
India | New Zealand | South Africa

Puffin Books is part of the Penguin Random House group of companies
whose addresses can be found at global.penguinrandomhouse.com.

www.penguin.co.uk   www.puffin.co.uk   www.ladybird.co.uk

Penguin
Random House
UK

First published 2018
001

Written by Chris Dixon and Ramsay Cudlipp
Text copyright © ChrisMD 2018
Illustrations by Dan Green
Illustrations copyright © Penguin Books Ltd 2018
The moral right of ChrisMD has been asserted

Printed in China

A CIP catalogue record for this book is available from the British Library

ISBN: 978–0–141–38771–0

All correspondence to:
Puffin Books
Penguin Random House Children's
80 Strand, London WC2R 0RL

Photography Credits
Thanks to Al Richardson and Ben Stevens
Photographs on pages 68, 69, 70, 72 copyright © Getty Images

The press cutting on page 66 has been reproduced with the
permission of the *Jersey Evening Post*

CHRISMD

Thrills, Skills and Molehills

contents

Throughout this book, you'll notice some of these:

These are QR codes linking straight to some of my favourite videos – including exclusive, never-before-seen stuff that I've recorded especially for this book.

Here's your quick-start guide on how to use them:

1. Using your smartphone or tablet, head to the app store and download a QR code reader. There are loads of free ones to choose from (and some devices already have a reader included).

2. You'll now be able to scan the QR code through your device's camera.

3. You'll be taken straight to the video, where you can watch it as often as you like!

It's as easy as that!

Welcome

Eugh. That's cheesy in written form. Far too cheesy. Instead, I'll just say . . .

How's it going? Welcome to my book!

It's all about everything I do, the beautiful game and, of course, the not so beautiful parts of it.

I do feel a little sorry for my family for the amount of football books and magazines they've had to buy me over the years, so here's one on me, Dad.

I've put a lot of effort into making this the football book I always wanted to read, so I hope you all have as much fun reading it as I did making it for you.

Enjoy!

Chris

17 Most goals scored in a season

4 Headers scored

12 Hat-tricks scored

1 'Perfect' hat-tricks scored (left foot, right foot, header)

6 Penalties converted

3 Penalties missed

1 Teams captained

4 Most goals scored in one match

2 Goals assisted by my dad

3 Assists provided for my dad

0 Yellow cards received

0 Red cards received

5 Teams played for in Jersey

1 Cup finals played where my dad was managing

1 Times subbed off in a cup final by my dad (Parenting 101)

WHO IS CHRIS MD?

10

Full name: Christopher Michael Dixon

Birthplace: Jersey, Channel Islands

Date of birth: 10 June 1996

Weight: 10.5 stone *10.4 without hair gel*

Height: 5 ft 8 in *If I'm wearing football boots. That's how everyone measures it, right?*

Shoe size: 7 *Cue general hilarity in shops when you're told they don't stock anything smaller than an 8.*

Favourite meal: Roast chicken

First car: Peugeot 207

Current car: Audi TT

Dream car: Audi R8 *Though it would be a bit pointless in Jersey, unless you particularly enjoy accelerating up to our maximum speed limit of 40 mph!*

Favourite holiday destination:
The Lake District *It's beautiful there, just one of those places that feels like holidays to me.*

FUN FACT

Even though we're from Jersey, we've always spent every single Christmas in the Lake District (that always gets a gasp!). It was also the shoot location for the infamous Nerf Wars which, come to think about it, probably isn't a good thing.

Favourite team: Arsenal

Second favourite team: Leeds

Lots of my relations support them.

Earliest memory: Playing football in the sitting room with my dad and sister.

Or, more specifically, belting rockets against our French window curtains and destroying entire shelves of ornaments as I won the World Cup in my own little world every evening.

Favourite football position: Central attacking midfield

I like playing in a role where I'm creating and scoring goals. And the lack of defensive responsibility is a nice bonus, I guess.

Favourite colour: Blue

I know it's controversial, but hey, Arsenal sometimes play in a blue away kit, and have blue on their badge, so . . .

Favourite band: Green Day

The first album I bought was 'American Idiot'. You just can't beat it.

Favourite time of day: Dawn

Hear me out! Although it doesn't happen often, I just love the feeling of having the entire day ahead of you (even if that day then consists of returning to bed until midday!).

Favourite comedian: Michael McIntyre

Even though he's a Spurs fan!

Favourite film: *The Lord of the Rings: Return of the King*

I'll go as far as to say 'LOTR' is the closest thing to a religion I have! However, none of this regular three-hour version rubbish. You want the full HD extended 'Return of the King'. The best four hours you'll ever spend.

Favourite instrument: Guitar

I've been playing for seven years! The 'Hotel California' solo by The Eagles is probably the most impressive thing I can play, but that's for another video someday . . .

Role model: Thierry Henry

A gentleman on and off the pitch. Not to mention his incredibly soothing pundit voice. *French accent* It . . . makes . . . him . . . sound . . . very . . . intelligent.

Favourite TV show: Game of Thrones

Definitely for the older audience, but I love that they are not afraid to kill off characters or have big twists in the story. They do things other shows wouldn't even dare to think of. That's why it's so gripping.

YOUTUBE ALLSTARS

1 **Marcus Butler**

2 **Calfreezy**

3 **JMX**

4 **Josh Pieters**

5 **Reev**

6 **ComedyShortsGamer**

7 **Callux**

8 **AnEsonGib**

9 **Me!**

10 **Castro1021**

11 **Hughwizzy**

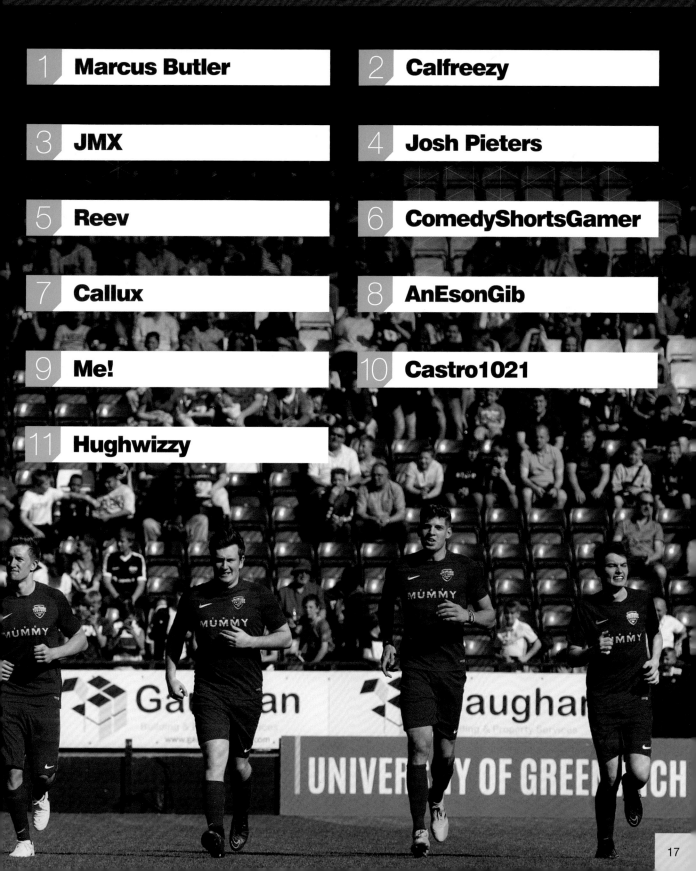

Family Album 1

I was never really sure if Dad had a child because he wanted a son, or he wanted a goalkeeper.

Boff!

Once I stopped trying to eat the ball, things became a lot easier.

I'm really quite proud of my parents' commitment to the Arsenal indoctrination. What chance did I have?

This is a funny-shaped football.

Rude

— that was the best day of your life.

Ah, glad you could join me, Kelly. (From this point on, she'll be helping me narrate these photos.)

I was never really sure if Dad had a second child because he wanted a daughter, or a football.

My YouTube Journey

The Nerf Wars

Uploaded: **2010**

Subscriber count: **0**

The first videos that I ever uploaded to YouTube. We would steal my parents' video camera and disappear for a few hours to record some cinematic gold!

CoD: Black Ops: No-Scope Montage L96A1

Uploaded: **Feb 2011**

Subscriber count: **53**

Probably one of the worst 'no-scope' montages ever. It consists of me going up to people who are about a yard away and shooting them in the back of the head. Impressive stuff.

Best Pack Ever!! 2 Informs + Ronaldo

Uploaded: **Sep 2011**

Subscriber count: **268**

The first video where I spoke. Looking back, I'm not quite sure why I decided that my first words to the world should be 'So, yeah . . .'.

The 4* Skilled Bronze Players – England *FIFA 12*

Uploaded: **Nov 2011**

Subscriber count: **289**

The first video that really earned me some subscribers. It got about 90,000 views quite quickly. I spent a lot of time editing this video and was really proud of it. This is when I started to realize how many people wanted to watch videos like this.

Earning 1,000 Subscribers

Date: **Aug 2012**

I was on holiday with my family in Italy at the time and I remember saying to Kelly: 'imagine 1,000 people in a room – they're all subscribed to me'. It's when I really started to think that this could actually lead somewhere.

WHY, EA?! | *FIFA 13* Funny Fail

Uploaded: **Nov 2012**

Subscriber count: **1,064**

The first time I ever showed my face on my channel. *FIFA* glitched when I scored but for some reason it gave a goal kick and this was my angry reaction. I pretended to destroy an old controller by unscrewing it and putting some screws in it so it 'broke' when I threw it down.

FIFA 14 | Double Touch Spin Tutorial

Uploaded: **Sep 2013**

Subscriber count: **1,967**

This was when I changed my name from Sirhcchris2010 to ChrisMD, having realized that I didn't really want to spend the rest of my life with everyone calling me 'Sir Chris'. VERY good decision.

20K Subscribers Special! – Scoring A Goal IRL

Uploaded: **Jan 2014**

Subscriber count: **20,034**

The first-ever video of me playing in a real game. I think this video shows how much I've changed in the last four years. Things were taking off at this point but I didn't think it would be enough.

100K Q&A

Uploaded: **Jun 2014**

Subscriber count: **116,897**

Kelly's first appearance! Some excellent acting from her, as she pretends to be punched by me. This video came out just at the end of my exams when I was still planning to train to be a vet. I was going to try to run my channel at the same time as studying, but I'm not sure it would have worked.

FOOTBALL CHALLENGES

Uploaded: **Aug 2014**

Subscriber count: **139,612**

I remember thinking that 'FOOTBALL CHALLENGES' was a really poor name at the time . . . My opinion has not changed. This was also Ollie's first appearance as a goalkeeper in a video. We filmed it in Germany, which is why I'm wearing my dad's trainers. Cringe. So. Much. Cringe.

The Decision Not to Go to Uni

Aug 2014

This is where I took a gap year to focus on my channel and to see how it went. It's fair to say it went better than expected.

Chris Dixon ✔
@chrismd10

Rejected my Nottingham Uni offer. Time to give this YouTube thing a real shot.

14/08/2014, 11:08

My Sunday League Season | 2013/14

Uploaded: **Nov 2014**

Subscriber count: **189,644**

My last season in junior football coincided with a few of our better players moving on. Consequently some of my, er, less gifted mates were brought in. I knew that people had to see this. I think I was one of the first people to do anything about Sunday League football and it's been a great success. People loved this video (well, apart from some of the less fortunate players featured) and I really enjoyed making it.

200K Q&A

Uploaded: **Nov 2014**

Subscriber count: **206,961**

I'm still proud of this one. It was quite a milestone, considering I'd gone from 2,500 subscribers to 200,000 in a year. It also features me doing some quite epic keepy-ups.

FIFA 15 – The Draft THE FINAL vs Zerkaa

Uploaded: **Dec 2014**

Subscriber count: **277,285**

This was the first time I'd ever really spoken to anyone big in the YouTube community. I remember being on a Skype call with Calfreezy and a few of the Sidemen and I was so nervous that I barely spoke! Don't tell them that – I was never a fanboy as far as they're concerned.

WEMBLEY CUP 2015 FOOTGOLF

When: **May 2015**

The first time I'd recorded in person with other YouTubers. Looking back at me and Manny in particular, you can see just how much we've changed in the last few years. Fun fact: Manny's the only person I've ever met to be born on EXACTLY the same day as me.

SCORING A SCREAMER AT WEMBLEY

Uploaded: **Aug 2015**

Subscriber count: **775,212**

The biggest perk of my YouTube career at this point. We were told we weren't allowed to slide-tackle on the pitch, which also meant that I couldn't do a knee slide when I scored. That's why my celebration was so bad. Honestly.

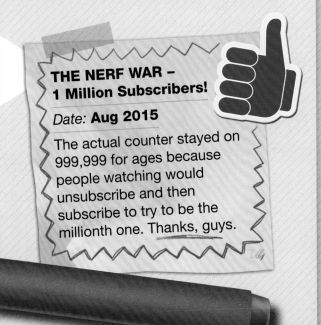

THE NERF WAR – 1 Million Subscribers!

Date: **Aug 2015**

The actual counter stayed on 999,999 for ages because people watching would unsubscribe and then subscribe to try to be the millionth one. Thanks, guys.

The Ultimate Sunday League Footballer vs Miniminter

Uploaded: **Dec 2015**

Subscriber count: **1,358,631**

My first video with Simon, having met him at the Wembley Cup, and Tobi (who was in goal). It was great of him to make a video with me, because he had so many more subscribers at the time. I was very much the newcomer to the London YouTube community, but luckily they couldn't be a nicer bunch of guys!

THE BEST 24 HOURS OF MY LIFE?!

Uploaded: **Feb 2016**

Subscriber count: **1,549,112**

This was incredible. JJ (KSI) very kindly bought an executive box at Arsenal vs Barcelona for loads of YouTubers. As you do. Despite the result, it was an absolutely unforgettable evening and I got to see Messi in the flesh. Plus, in the space of the same 24 hours, I finally had my braces taken off! I started to smile a lot more in my videos after that.

JERSEY VS GUERNSEY | FOOTBALL CHALLENGES ft. WROETOSHAW

Uploaded: **Mar 2016**

Subscriber count: **1,654,867**

My most popular video and also my favourite. It took four days of solid editing but it was worth it. Watching Harry jump into my swimming pool as a punishment for losing was very satisfying. I get the feeling I may not have earned many Guernsey subscribers, though.

THE 2ND NERF WAR – 2 Million Subscribers!

Date: **June 2016**

No one was around to celebrate this with me because it was so early in the morning and they were at work or school. I got up early to watch it, though. (I don't get out of bed for anything less than two million subscribers.)

The Sidemen Football Match

June 2016

The first game we'd played in front of a big crowd. Walking out of the tunnel (fashionably late, of course) is something I'll remember for the rest of my life. That's probably the best moment of my YouTube career so far.

A MESSI PENALTY IN FRONT OF 500,000

Uploaded: **Jun 2016**

Subscriber count: **2,091,345**

It's sort of become a tradition to dissect my performances after these games. It's like a Sunday League season video, but on a slightly different stage! Got to use that penalty clickbait opportunity, though. You know how it is.

THE BEST-EVER EURO GOALS RE-CREATION BATTLE VS MY DAD

Uploaded: **Jul 2016**

Subscriber count: **2,243,961**

The first time I'd filmed a video with my dad. It was nice to pay him back, seeing as he's taught me everything I know about football. Well, most things I know about football. Or maybe just a few things. In fact, I've probably taught him more than he's taught me.

BATTLING AGAINST MY CHILDHOOD HERO

Date: **Sep 2016**

Subscriber count: **2,342,115**

The second Wembley Cup, and my first game playing with professional footballers. Lining up against Robert Pires was INCREDIBLE, and the Wembley atmosphere was insane. This was also the game where Kelly and Ollie got mobbed by fans!

MOTHER VS SON
The Ultimate Football Battle

Uploaded: **Jan 2017**

Subscriber count: **2,881,371**

My dad had already featured a few times so it was nice to bring Mum in as a way of saying thanks. Oh, and she'd been complaining that she hadn't been featured. To be fair, she is much better than Dad on camera. A natural star. And she beat us all hands down in this challenge!

Visiting Abu Dhabi with Manchester City

Date: **Feb 2017**

Subscriber count: **2,993,458**

This was an incredible opportunity. I went with Simon (Miniminter) and the break it gave us was an added bonus (he's probably the hardest-working guy I've ever met). We just about put up with each other for four days.

3,000,321

The 3rd & Final Nerf War – 3 MILLION SUBSCRIBERS

Date: **Feb 2017**

I actually missed this moment because me and Simon were out having a romantic dinner in Abu Dhabi. And I couldn't go out and celebrate because I had to get up early the next day to film with the Man City players. (That's not a sentence you write every day . . .) Don't worry, though. J-Town (or 'Jersey' as some people know it) was the perfect place to celebrate my milestone the following week.

FILMING AT THE ARSENAL TRAINING GROUND

Uploaded: **Apr 2017**

Subscriber count: **3,124,426**

A dream come true. Finally I'd been called up to the Arsenal training ground! Yeah, all right, maybe not in the circumstances I'd dreamed of ten years ago . . . but I'll take it. I filmed with five players on the day, including one Alexis Sanchez (who had never filmed with anyone on YouTube before).

MEETING CRISTIANO RONALDO

Uploaded: **Sep 2017**

Subscriber count: **3,567,798**

This is still an achievement that I cannot get my head around. This one really takes the biscuit. Ronaldo was the reigning winner of the Ballon d'Or (whether or not I agree with that!), which made him the best player in the world. Never mind meeting him, I FILMED WITH the best player in the world. Seriously – how do I ever top this? Oh wait, I know . . .

WELCOME TO THE FORTRESS

15

12

16

3 • 14

7

1

5

6

1 First goal scored

This was on the junior pitch when I was playing for St John Primary School A team. There was no offside rule, so you could goal-hang like there was no tomorrow. Those were the days! I had a good 10 yards on the defenders as the ball was played through, before slotting it into the bottom left corner. Clinical.

2 The bushes

I must have spent half of my life retrieving footballs from these bushes.

3 World Cup Singles/Doubles arena

The World Cup Singles or Doubles goal of choice (see page 151). Also the goal in which I spent days on end playing with my dad when I was very young. You could say I taught him everything he knows about football.

4 The greenhouse

I clearly remember someone hitting a failed overhead kick from the middle of the junior pitch which somehow hit this greenhouse. To be fair, any houses within 500 yards were at risk when we were shooting.

5 The forgotten pitch roller

There has been a huge pitch roller in this corner of the field for as long as I can remember. But I don't think it's ever been used (which probably explains why the pitch is so bumpy). One day I'll get hold of a tractor and try to roll the pitch with it. One day!

6 The worst floodlights in history

Playing under these is like trying to play football by candlelight. In winter, the training area at The Fortress is basically the size of a squash court because the floodlights aren't bright enough to light up anything bigger.

7 Molehills

If the moles have been particularly busy, it means that no one can physically play on the wings because it's like running through a World War One potato field. I've been tackled by molehills more times than by defenders in my career. Sometimes kick-off is delayed as the players have to stamp them flat. It's a great warm-up.

8 The dugouts

These really are quite special. They're falling apart, don't even have seats any more (or a roof) and they offer no protection from the elements at all – not to mention the rabid dog in the garden behind you, which is separated from the dugouts by a worryingly thin fence (as if we don't have enough hazards to watch out for during a Sunday League match!).

9 The stand

It has a 'capacity' of around fifty but I've never known more than about six people to be up there. It does have one of the best views for watching football in Jersey, however, even if the standard on the pitch is not always all that high.

10 My tennis injury

This is now a skate park but for years it was two tennis courts – where a great story of mine was once born. I was taking part in a few practice serves in the first 30 seconds of a tennis match when the racket flew out of my hand, bounced off the tarmac and smacked me in the forehead. Not one of my prouder moments. There was a lot of blood and I still have the scar. I generally tell people it's from fighting a shark.

11 My best goal at The Fortress

I scored an absolute rocket from here. One of our current goalkeepers was in the sticks, playing for a different team at the time, which made it even sweeter.

12 Carrot disaster

I was filming a video with YouTuber Harry (W2S) using chocolate carrots when suddenly a load of kids turned up for a primary school football match so we had to move. I felt quite sorry for the poor goalkeeper who had to stand in all the carrot debris we'd left behind from the challenge. It wasn't as if the already-bumpy six-yard box needed any more obstructions!

13 The sports hall

Nowadays everyone suffers grazed knees on 3G plastic pitches, but when I was growing up we had something even worse – carpet. We used to train in this hall in winter when the outside pitch was ruined, and after ten minutes no one had any skin left on their legs. Or hope.

14 The triple finish

This was the scene of one of my best footballing moments caught on video. It was during a challenge when Ollie was in goal and I scored three screamers in a row. Poor Ollie might not want to see this again but I never tire of watching it! I particularly enjoyed Ollie's comment: 'if anyone wants to be Chris's cousin, there's a free space'. Cousinly love, eh?

15 My dad's flukey goal/cross

My dad scored possibly the flukiest goal ever from this spot. He says it was a shot. OKAY, MATE.

16 ▶ First crossbar challenge

I do love a crossbar challenge and I like to think I've got better over the last few years. I was injured doing my first attempt so had to do it left-footed, which meant that it probably took a bit longer to film than some of my other videos!

17 ▶ Football graveyard

I've kicked hundreds of balls over the fence behind this goal and normally I find them in the end. But if they land in this thick, prickly hedge, it's all over. It's like stepping into Narnia.

18 ▶ The outside 'toilet'

The spot where players would always take a pre-match wee because the inside toilets were so bad. The changing rooms were actually refurbished last season but there are a few players who still make a pre-match stop out here. Shout-out to those lads – you're the real heroes.

19 ▶ Dog poo danger zone

It only takes one big Labrador to ruin a game of football. This is a particularly dodgy area for some reason. One of our games was delayed for about fifteen minutes once because everyone was arguing over whose job it was to clear it up! I wish I was joking.

20 ▶ The gantry

Various cameramen and women have filmed my games from the 'media box' (an old picnic bench) up here. Unfortunately, the new youth club extension slightly obscures the bottom corner of the pitch these days. It's a shame, because that's where I pulled off that sombrero-flick-to-rainbow-flick combo before smashing it into the top corner that one time. Honest.

Family Album 2

Finally, I have a ball at my feet – even if it comes up to my knees.

When someone takes away my football

And your reaction is still the same all these years later!

Time to introduce another member of the family. Anyone spot a familiar face? No, not Master Yoda — Ollie!

AND THE REST IS HISTORY.

Kelly, Ollie and me, enjoying a day out in the playground.

If I push her hard enough, she may reach the pond yet . . .

I'm sure that's Chris's hand I can feel on my back . . .

CHRIS'S MATCH DAY EXPERIENCE

(Ideal World)

8 a.m.
Alarm goes off.

8.01 a.m.
Get out of bed.

8.15 a.m.
Prepare and consume a smoothie (banana, strawberry, oats).

8.30 a.m.
Light jog around the block and some gentle stretching.

9.00 a.m.
Pitch inspection at The Fortress to examine firmness of the turf and decide whether or not mouldies or studs are required.

9.15 a.m.
Eat a small bowl of porridge and fruit.

9.30 a.m.
Quick shower.

10 a.m.
Start styling hair.

11 a.m.
Finish styling hair.

10.30 a.m.
Continue styling hair.

11.15 a.m.
Sports massage from physiotherapist to loosen up leg muscles.

12.00 p.m.
Light lunch of pasta, tuna and vegetables.

12.30 p.m.
Arrive at the pitch and set up some cones for the warm-up. Make sure that the number 10 shirt is not taken. Hire local thugs to deal with the situation if it is.

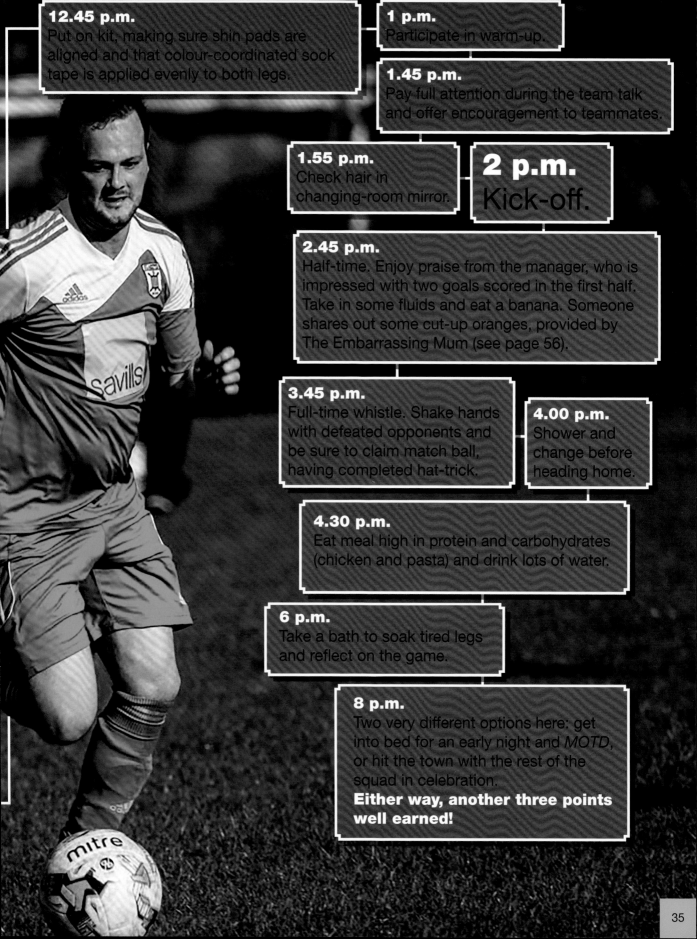

12.45 p.m.
Put on kit, making sure shin pads are aligned and that colour-coordinated sock tape is applied evenly to both legs.

1 p.m.
Participate in warm-up.

1.45 p.m.
Pay full attention during the team talk and offer encouragement to teammates.

1.55 p.m.
Check hair in changing-room mirror.

2 p.m.
Kick-off.

2.45 p.m.
Half-time. Enjoy praise from the manager, who is impressed with two goals scored in the first half. Take in some fluids and eat a banana. Someone shares out some cut-up oranges, provided by The Embarrassing Mum (see page 56).

3.45 p.m.
Full-time whistle. Shake hands with defeated opponents and be sure to claim match ball, having completed hat-trick.

4.00 p.m.
Shower and change before heading home.

4.30 p.m.
Eat meal high in protein and carbohydrates (chicken and pasta) and drink lots of water.

6 p.m.
Take a bath to soak tired legs and reflect on the game.

8 p.m.
Two very different options here: get into bed for an early night and *MOTD*, or hit the town with the rest of the squad in celebration.
Either way, another three points well earned!

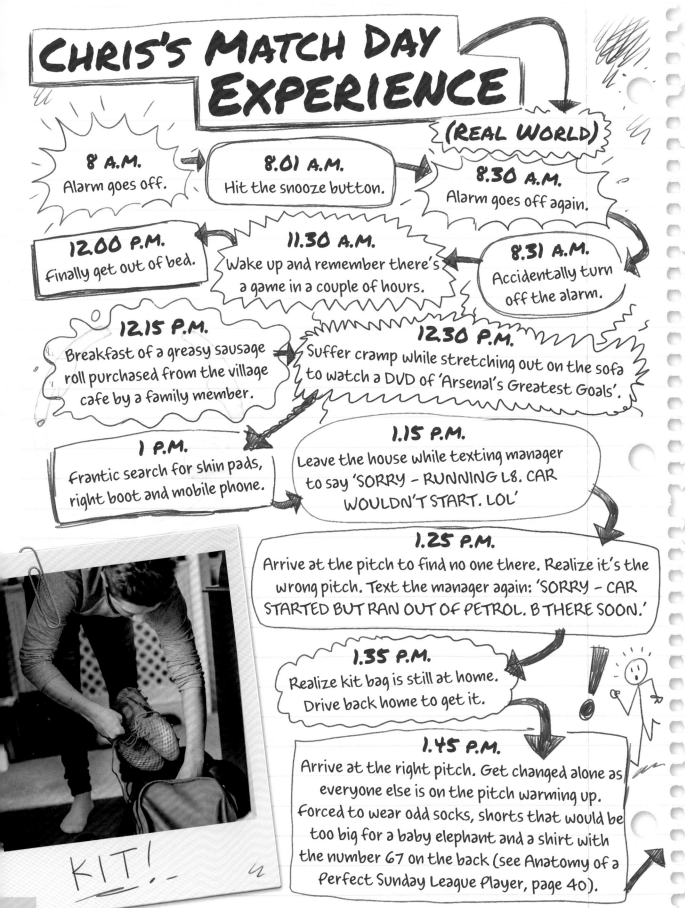

CHRIS'S MATCH DAY EXPERIENCE
(REAL WORLD)

8 A.M.
Alarm goes off.

8.01 A.M.
Hit the snooze button.

8.30 A.M.
Alarm goes off again.

8.31 A.M.
Accidentally turn off the alarm.

11.30 A.M.
Wake up and remember there's a game in a couple of hours.

12.00 P.M.
Finally get out of bed.

12.15 P.M.
Breakfast of a greasy sausage roll purchased from the village cafe by a family member.

12.30 P.M.
Suffer cramp while stretching out on the sofa to watch a DVD of 'Arsenal's Greatest Goals'.

1 P.M.
Frantic search for shin pads, right boot and mobile phone.

1.15 P.M.
Leave the house while texting manager to say 'SORRY – RUNNING L8. CAR WOULDN'T START. LOL'

1.25 P.M.
Arrive at the pitch to find no one there. Realize it's the wrong pitch. Text the manager again: 'SORRY – CAR STARTED BUT RAN OUT OF PETROL. B THERE SOON.'

1.35 P.M.
Realize kit bag is still at home. Drive back home to get it.

1.45 P.M.
Arrive at the right pitch. Get changed alone as everyone else is on the pitch warming up. Forced to wear odd socks, shorts that would be too big for a baby elephant and a shirt with the number 67 on the back (see Anatomy of a Perfect Sunday League Player, page 40).

KIT!

1.55 P.M.
Just enough time to fire a few balls at the goalkeeper (but all three fly over the bar and into the bushes).

2.05 P.M.
Kick-off is delayed as both teams search for the missing balls.

2.10 P.M.
KICK-OFF.

2.55 P.M.
Half-time. Am singled out for blame for three of the five goals that have already been conceded. No one remembered to bring the oranges. (Shots attempted by me: 7. Shots on target: 0. Shots that went out for a throw-in: 3.)

OOF!

3.55 P.M.
Full-time. The manager left five minutes before the end of the 10-0 defeat (so missed my last-minute own goal).

4.10 P.M.
Head straight home after a cold shower.

6.30 P.M.
Suffer cramp in the bath and get stuck in the same position for two hours cos no one is around to hear my screams.

6 P.M.
No real food in the house, so forced to eat a bowl of cereal for dinner.

10.30 P.M.
Watch 'Match of the Day' to find out that Arsenal lost 1-0 at home to a team in the relegation zone.

11.45 P.M.
Finally go to bed.

DOH!

11.46 P.M.
Fall asleep thinking about that own goal.

ZZZ

My Attributes . . .

ChrisMD

CAM

PACE: 85

PASSING: 94

SHOOTING: 83

A lot of people put my shooting in the 90s when rating my footballing ability. Somewhere between 91 and 99 would seem accurate . . . depending on how much editing of my videos I've done, that is. Funnily enough, it may be a little lower, having watched the uncut versions of certain videos!

DRIBBLING: 91

I'm still a good dribbler, however, and I back my passing even higher, if you'll allow me to be totally immodest for a moment.

DEFENDING: 71

I do actually tackle quite a lot, now that my younger years are behind me and I'm not half the height of the no-nonsense centre-back on the other team.

PHYSICAL: 70

I'm still waiting to be booked, which would really be a perfect addition to my Sunday League accolades. I need to get my act together!

MY SUNDAY LEAGUE ATTRIBUTES...

CHRIS MD

THROW-INS: 55

I've always played in the middle of the pitch so bicep-busting 100 m Rory Delap throw-ins aren't a weapon I bring out very often.

CRUNCHING TACKLES: 75

I do love a crunching tackle. I think I get away with it because I don't really have a face that says 'you're not going to be using those legs again'. Well, not unless someone asks me if I've been practising penalties.

BALL RETRIEVAL: 95

I've had a LOT of practice at this from hunting for footballs in the 'Amazon rainforest' of bushes behind my team's home ground (or 'The Fortress' as it's universally known).

STAND-IN GOALKEEPING: 3

I haven't been graced with the privilege (yet) of being a stand-in goalkeeper (see page 62). Luckily (for me), that job usually goes to a lanky centre-back.

BOOT GAME: 80

ROW Z CLEARANCES: 10

It frustrates plenty of the 'English-bred' defenders I've played with, but I'll never hoof the ball away to safety, even in my own penalty area with five players around me! Rainbow flicks may be pushing it though. But still funny.

CAM

Anatomy of a Perfect Sunday League Player

HINDSIGHT
Knowing what your teammate should have done with the ball, just after he's given it away. (He should have passed to you, obviously.)

VISION OF AN EAGLE
The ability to see offside better than the ref's assistant, even though you're at the other end of the pitch and he's in line with play. No-nonsense centre-backs always seem to possess this ability.

NECKLACE
There's always someone who tries to get round the 'no jewellery' rule. An easy way to spot a Twinkle-Toes (see page 60).

SHIRT
Always too big for most players, the shirts must be made of thick nylon (perfect for summer games!) and they must have extra-long sleeves, as well as the capacity to soak up water until they're double their original weight.

HAIR
This slightly messy style is a result of 'bed head', having only woken up 20 minutes before kick-off and not showered since the night out before.

FOREHEAD
The ball is in the air a lot during amateur football (mainly because the pitches are so bumpy) so you need to be able to cope with lots of headers. A strong forehead doesn't go amiss when a member of the opposition squares up to you for daring to try a Panenka penalty, too.

GLOVES
It may be the middle of September but if your hero (Luis Suarez, Sergio Aguero or . . . er . . . Marouane Fellaini) can wear them, so can you.

CAPTAIN'S ARMBAND
Always made from the tape everyone else uses to hold up their socks. The real armband is almost always lost during the second game of the season when the captain angrily throws it in the bin after being substituted.

ST JOHNS

F.C.

CAPTAIN

BRUISE

This perfectly round, red bruise is the unmistakable mark of a player who has been on the receiving end of a centre-back's failed clearance. Or even worse, they're one of the unlucky cannon-fodder group who were shouted at to get in the wall. R.I.P.

SOCKS

These are never a matching pair, especially if you turn up late. One will definitely have a big hole in it and if you're lucky they might be similar shades of the same colour. One is so big that opposition players might get caught in it when trying to tackle you, and the other is so small it cuts off blood circulation to the leg, meaning that a second ambulance has to be called (the first one turned up after a fight between the managers).

SHIN PADS

You've forgotten your shin pads (again). Don't worry – a cardboard takeaway coffee cup is a perfect substitute! Tear it into two halves and tuck them inside your socks to make it look as if you are wearing pads.

SHORTS

These must always hinder running ability in some way. Either they're so massive that ninety per cent of your time and energy is spent pulling them up, or so small that they look like hot pants.

MUSCLE RUB

Every changing room smells of this stuff, which everyone applies generously to the back of their legs. Most people use it instead of doing a warm-up. No one knows where it has come from as no one has ever actually bought any. Does it regenerate in the bottom of old first-aid kits? Does it actually do anything?

GOOD LEFT FOOT

Everyone knows someone who is described as having a 'good left foot'. What this actually means is that they are useless at football but once accidentally hit a cross that ended up in the top corner on a windy day. They will also demand to take every free kick, despite failing to hit the target 17 times in a row since 2009.

BOOTS

These need to be as colourful as possible, making you look like someone who means business. (However, they also need to be slightly muddy.)

Chris's Top Five Challenges with Footballers

5.

THE COMPLETE PENALTY CHALLENGE VS YAYA TOURE

When: November 2016

Where: Manchester City's training ground. Being able to play there was amazing. It's nearly as good as The Fortress. Nearly.

Why: Manchester City invited me to film some football content with Yaya (yeah, we're on first-name terms).

Who won? We didn't really have a winner, but I'd say it was definitely me! Well, I scored the best penalty on the day – a rabona into the bottom corner. Tell me it gets better than that! (Well, other than a rabona into the top corner.)

Unknown fact: We were waiting near the reception before filming the video when Pep Guardiola walked in. He was just a few metres away and said 'morning' to us, like it was totally normal. I was one of just five people who were there in the room to reply 'morning' back to him that day. Hear that? One of five people! Save that one for the grandkids! (I've just re-read this part and I'm not even sure if I'm joking.)

Yaya was probably the nicest guy I've ever made a video with. I've never known anyone who laughs so much! He wasn't allowed to kick the ball too hard (in case he got injured!) but he seemed to really enjoy himself. He's another footballer who was totally down to earth and didn't just turn up with the attitude that he was there because he had to be. In return (and also because he's 6 ft 2 in), I made no birthday cake jokes.

4.

Chris vs Simon
THE SHOOT-OUT Ft. De Bruyne, Sterling, Sané & Caballero

When: April 2017

Where: Abu Dhabi

Why: YouTuber Miniminter (Simon) and I were invited to join Manchester City on a training break.

Who won? My team won, of course! (Although that might have had something to do with my team including Sterling and De Bruyne.)

Unknown fact: We had to change the challenge at the last minute because the large goals we needed weren't delivered in time. The small goals we had would have made it too easy for a professional keeper – so that's why we all took it in turns playing in goal (and also why Willy Caballero was blasting rockets all over the place instead of saving them).

This trip was nothing short of incredible. We stayed in one of the best hotels in the world (sorry, we stayed in a palace!) and got to play football with some of the world's most famous football players (I'm sure they were just as excited to see us, too . . .). Raheem was a great guy and, again, he spoke to us just like a mate. Players like that are incredibly easy to make great videos with because the comedy is all there already without needing three days of editing! Which is nice.

3.

ChrisMD vs ALEXIS SANCHEZ, HOLDING & ELNENY
Impossible Goal Line Shooting

When: April 2017

Where: Arsenal's Training Ground, London

Why: I'd heard word of an opportunity to film with five Arsenal players, so I wasn't going to let that one go!

Who won? Well . . . in my video . . . not me. Unfortunately, we'd decided before the video that my challenge with Carl Jenkinson and Gabriel would be an exclusive for Dugout's website, which made my video a difficult edit after I lost all three challenges to Alexis Sanchez, Rob Holding and Mohamed Elneny!

Unknown fact: I didn't actually know if I'd get to film with Alexis until he walked over to us on the day. I was guaranteed five Arsenal players to film with, but Mustafi got swapped out late on for Jenkinson and suddenly there was no guarantee I'd get to film with Alexis either.

Extra unknown fact: I said in the video that we couldn't play 'Rock, Paper, Scissors' with Alexis because of the language barrier. What actually happened is we played it, I won, then he took the first kick anyway. What am I supposed to do in that situation? Ask him if he knows who I am?

'I'd heard word of an opportunity to film with five Arsenal players, so I wasn't going to let that one go!'

From Aaron Ramsey jogging past me in the car park to Steve Bould driving by in his ten-year-old BMW 'dad car', this was a pretty surreal day. It was also the day after we got smashed 3-0 at Crystal Palace, so before I'd even turned up things were going pretty poorly. Luckily, the players who joined me were perfect on-screen. Rob Holding was the pick of the bunch, immediately making it feel like a kickabout with one of my mates. I bumped into him later in reception and he asked me how I had got on. It's a great feeling when you seem to have actually made an impression on players for the good, rather than them just seeing it as another boring media duty. Still waiting for the Arsène Wenger collab though. I'm thinking '30-yard Overhead Kick Challenge'.

2.

CRISTIANO RONALDO Reacts to My Football Videos

When: September 2017

Where: Madrid, Spain

Why: This is a real story for the grandkids. So one day an email arrived from CR7's agency, asking if I'd be interested in making content with him . . . genuinely!

Who won? Well, there's not really any way in which Cristiano could have lost . . . but I certainly feel like I won, considering I'm now the proud owner of two football boots signed by him.

Unknown fact: His agency hadn't actually fully approved him watching and rating my football videos, but they hadn't said 'no' either. I just had to trust my judgement on the day and try to pitch him the idea in the seven minutes we had. Luckily for me, he loved it and one of the people from his agency told me he'd enjoyed it the most out of all the media shoots he'd done that day!

I've met loads of my idols through my job over the last few years, so I reckon I don't get star-struck all that easily. This guy, however . . . Cristiano had an entourage of a good twenty people and security guards at all times. He seemed like such a nice guy, and was joking with us off camera and checking on how we were. It was refreshing to see someone with his profile still giving out so much respect to everyone. Which was good for him, or my first question might have been, 'Which of Messi's Ballon d'Or wins was your favourite?'

Thinking about it, that was probably good for me too. My survival rate after dropping that wouldn't have been very high.

1.

FOOTBALL CHALLENGES WITH THE WORLD'S BEST GOALKEEPERS (Kelly and Ollie!)

When: September 2016

Where: The Fortress, Jersey

Why: To give Kelly and Ollie a chance to redeem themselves between the sticks.

Who won? I won. Easily. It wasn't even close. That's right, you two. WASN'T EVEN CLOSE.

Unknown fact: It was meant to be Kelly and Ollie competing against each other, but in the end we just couldn't get a good save out of either of them to use for the ending of the video. That's why we ended up finishing the video with me scoring a Tony Yeboah-esque volley!

Although they're often referred to as the two goalkeepers in the world who can rival Manuel Neuer, I've also given Ollie and Kelly a lot of abuse in the past so this was their opportunity to show off their skills. I wanted to test out how good they really were. This video did really well and I think it was down to how natural it all felt. The three of us have a great relationship. This was filmed just after the Wembley Cup, and they were bombarded by fans looking for photos and autographs. Never mind £50 million footballers – these two are the real celebrities!

Family Album 3

They know their place at the family computer.

Yes, as I stare on in awe and Ollie stares on in confusion.

Shame 'FIFA '99' isn't a two-player game. Oh, wait, it is.

Flying my home-made B-52 made of toilet rolls (I wasn't subtle with my Christmas present hints).

You spent far too long on that.

Flying the slightly better
B-52 my grandpa made.

*To be fair, that was a pretty
cool present. On another note,
why are you still wearing the
same top? This was definitely
taken on a different day.*

A football team isn't for a day,
Kelly. It's for a lifetime.
Apology accepted.

What else do you wear to play beach tennis
in Jersey other than full Arsenal away-kit?

*You were preparing for Wimbledon
but got confused with the kit.*

Feel sorry for whoever's
thrown that to me
from 1 yard out of
the picture.

It was probably me.

SUNDAY LEAGUE CHARACTERS

Wherever Sunday League football is played, from the frozen wastelands of Siberia to the sun-baked plains of Africa, I guarantee that you could turn up to any match and you would come across the following characters . . .

NO.1: THE PLAYER MANAGER

- Usually a player who is getting near the end of his playing days and has lost a bit of pace.

- Cleverly able to ensure he still gets picked in the team.

- Puts himself on penalty-taking duty.

- Ignores what he says in his own team talk about passing the ball and tries to dribble past the entire opposition.

- Normally plays himself in centre midfield (and may well give himself the captain's armband, too).

- Often pulls a muscle during the first five minutes because he spent the warm-up filling in the team sheet and pumping up the match ball.

- Only substitutes himself off the pitch if he has already scored or if the team are losing 4-0.

- Everyone always passes to him because they're scared of losing their places in the team.

Key attribute:
WASHING THE KIT
Sunday League value:
8/10

NO.2: THE MANAGER'S SON

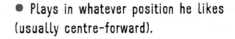

- Plays in whatever position he likes (usually centre-forward).

- Is always mentioned in the team talk by the manager, who tells everyone to pass him the ball.

- Never gets any abuse from the other players (even if he's been rubbish).

- Always has his kit on before anyone else because he's been at the ground with his dad for two hours setting up cones and jogging round the pitch.

- Always wins the manager's Player of the Year, regardless of how he has played.

- Whenever he goes down injured, his dad sprints on to the pitch with the medical bag to look after him . . .

- But he's only ever substituted if he has something serious, like a compound fracture.

- If he misses a game for any reason, his dad will dedicate the win to him.

Key attribute:
ATTENDANCE
(because his dad makes him)
Sunday League value:
7/10

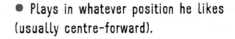

SUNDAY LEAGUE CHARACTERS

51

NO.3: THE GOODY TWO-SHOES

- Spends most of his life on the bench and hasn't started a game for three years.

- Fills up the water bottles before a game and helps hang up the kit.

- Ends up having to run the line and suffers more abuse from his own players than the opposition.

- The only person to have successfully paid his club's membership fees for the season (not this season – the one three seasons ago).

- Attends every training session, come rain or shine, and keenly listens to everything the coach has to say.

- Carries out a lengthy warm-up along the touchline for the duration of the game, even if he doesn't come on.

- Doesn't ever actually touch the ball more than three times while he is on the pitch.

Key attribute:
COLLECTING THE CONES
Sunday League value:
6/10

NO.4: THE ANGRY DAD

- Was a semi-professional player until an injury cut short his career.

- Abusive to everyone on the pitch, including the referee, despite it being an under-sevens friendly match.

- Everyone is a bit embarrassed by his behaviour, but no one is brave enough to confront him.

- If his team are winning 1-0 in the last minute of a cup final and an opposition player runs along the line with the ball, he won't be able to resist two-footing that player (even if they're a six-year-old).

- Always wears his old club tracksuit, which has his initials on the right side of the chest.

- Spends the whole drive home telling his son what he did wrong on the pitch, despite him scoring a hat-trick and winning Man of the Match.

Key attribute:
TELLING YOU HOW GOOD HE WAS AT FOOTBALL
Sunday League value:
8/10

NO. 5: THE GUY WHO SHOUTS A LOT IN THE CHANGING ROOM AT HALF-TIME

- Normally a centre-back, every team has that one player who approaches each game as if it was the Champions League final.

- NEVER engages in pre-game banter. Instead, he sits in silence, listening to 'Lose Yourself' by Eminem while imagining himself making epic last-ditch tackles.

- Shouts a lot in the changing room at half-time. And during the game. And after the game.

- Usually at fault for conceding the first goal, but manages to get around that by blaming everyone else.

- Does not seem to actually enjoy football. No one has seen him smile in six years.

- Heads absolutely everything, and loves nothing more than a strong 50/50 challenge.

- Strongly contests every red card he's ever had. Even that one that ended someone's career. Especially that one.

- If his team loses, he spends the next week in a bad mood.

Key attribute:
CRUNCHING TACKLES
Sunday League value:
9/10

NO.6: THE EMBARRASSING MUM

YAY!

- Spends the whole match screaming at the top of her voice, regardless of what is happening on the pitch.

- Very protective of her son and will loudly tell off any player who dares to kick him.

- Usually wears something that stands out, such as a hand-knitted jumper and bobble hat in the club colours.

- Tries to talk to the players as they leave the pitch at half-time, but everyone ignores her.

- Tends to miss any goals scored by her son because she is chatting with other parents or getting a cup of tea.

- When she does see a goal, she celebrates far too loudly (ruining any video footage someone may be trying to get from the game).

- Always brings the half-time oranges in a huge bag, even though everyone prefers sports drinks.

Key attribute:
CHATTING
Sunday League value:
10/10

NO.7: The Man Walking a Dog

- Always has a moustache, a raincoat and a hat. Always. Even if it's not raining.

- Used to play professional football for Portsmouth several decades ago and will chat about it to anyone who will listen.

- Never there at the start, but always arrives in the middle of the second half so he can approach someone and ask 'what's the score?'

- Chats to any other spectators and will often have a flask of tea, which he offers to share. No one accepts.

- Even though he is supposed to be walking his dog, he will always end up watching the match until the end.

- At some point the dog will escape from him and run across the pitch, chasing the ball. It will take ten minutes to recapture the mutt.

- Actually understands football better than anyone on the pitch and can quickly see why the home team are playing the wrong formation. (See page 120 for a guide to Sunday League formations.)

Key attribute:
LOOKING THE WRONG WAY AS HIS DOG FOULS AGAINST THE CORNER FLAG
Sunday League value:
8/10

NO.8: THE KIDS WHO DON'T SEEM TO BELONG TO ANYONE

- Usually a boy and a girl, between the ages of four and eight.

- No one knows who they're with or why they're there.

- Can always be seen playing by the touchline with a spare ball, which inevitably rolls on to the pitch. As a rule, they always choose to run on and collect it just as a 14-stone winger is hurtling towards them at full speed.

- They have absolutely no interest in the match, even if their dad is taking part.

- They are wearing replica Barcelona and Real Madrid kits, despite their parents being from Sheffield.

- Their afternoon always ends when one of them is struck in the face with a ball, and a furious parent appears from nowhere to take them home.

Key attribute:
STEALING MATCH BALLS
Sunday League value:
5/10

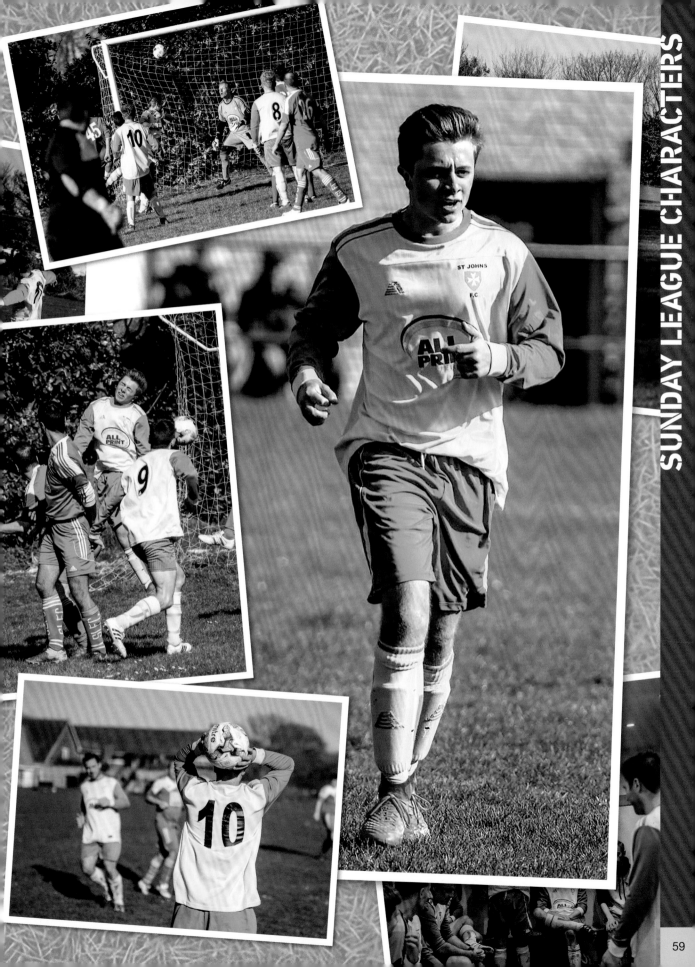

NO.9: TWINKLE-TOES

(A.K.A. THE WINGER WHO THINKS HE'S CRISTIANO RONALDO)

- Has slicked-back hair, a headband and an earring (covered up by a plaster).

- Always has the brightest, most expensive pair of boots (usually orange) and for some reason his kit always looks brand new.

- Spends the whole game sulking on the wing and shouting at his teammates to pass him the ball.

- When he does get possession, he tries so many step-overs that he trips himself up but still calls for a penalty (even if he's on the half-way line).

- Insists on taking every free-kick. Always adopts the Ronaldo stance (legs apart and arms at his side) before running up and smashing the ball into the stratosphere.

- Rolls around in agony clutching his knee when he's tackled, but is ignored by the opposition, the referee, his teammates and even The Man Walking a Dog (see page 57).

- If he's subbed, he gets his stuff from the changing room and goes home before the game is finished.

Key attribute:
STYLING HIS HAIR

Sunday League value:
9/10

THE GOALKEEPER'S MATE

- Always turns up halfway through the first half and is chuffed to find out that he knows the goalkeeper.

- Spends the rest of the game leaning on the post and chatting to his friend, completely distracting him.

- Accidentally draws the keeper to one side of the goal, leaving the opposition able to score from 50 yards out.

- Seems to have no concept of the fact that there is a football match taking place.

- Doesn't even retrieve the ball when it goes into the bushes behind the goal.

- Has to be told by the referee that he is too close to the pitch when a corner is being taken. Resumes his position as soon as the ball is cleared.

- Brings the goalkeeper a cup of tea, which he promptly spills as he tries to catch a cross seconds later.

BLAH BLAH BLAH

Key attribute:
LOTS OF SPARE TIME
Sunday League value:
6/10

NO.11: THE STAND-IN GOALKEEPER

- Usually one of the taller substitutes, or occasionally the Manager's Son (see page 51).

- Doesn't have any gloves, so is scared of making any saves or of catching the ball . . .

- But he does usually have a cap, for some reason, even if it isn't sunny.

- Usually wears someone's spare hoody instead of a keeper's top.

- Spends most of the game chatting to The Goalkeeper's Mate (see page 61).

- Doesn't move an inch from his line, even when a striker is one-on-one and running towards him.

- Despite all of his teammates promising before the game not to shout at him if he makes any mistakes, everyone turns against him when he manages to throw the ball into his own net.

- Refuses to take any goal kicks so one of the centre-backs has to help him out.

- Insists on someone swapping with him for the last ten minutes so he can go up front.

- Will make at least one ridiculously good save during an otherwise awful performance and bring it up in every conversation for the next six years.

Key attribute:
COMPLETELY FAILING TO GET HIS BODY BEHIND THE BALL
Sunday League value:
7/10

No.12: The Girlfriend Watching from the Sideline

- Always wearing sunglasses, whatever the weather, so no one can tell she's not really watching the game.

- Usually completely overdressed in high heels.

- Often leaves before the end of the game because she's annoyed that her boyfriend didn't speak to her at half-time.

- Only stays for the second 45 minutes if her boyfriend skips the half-time team talk to find her because he's worried one of his teammates will hit on her.

- Spends most of the game on her phone texting her friends about how good her boyfriend looks in shorts.

- Puzzled that her boyfriend is not the best player in the team, which is what he's been telling her for weeks.

- Always by herself because she couldn't persuade anyone to spend a Sunday morning watching a poor game of amateur football.

- All of the players are very aware of her presence and make an extra effort to perform tricks in her honour, especially Twinkle-Toes (see page 60).

Key attribute:
TEXTING AVIDLY
Sunday League value:
3/10

NO.13: THE VOLUNTEER LINESMAN

● While most games have an official referee, the linesmen are nearly always 'volunteers' (i.e. very unwilling substitutes who have been promised a whole second half on the pitch in return for running the line).

● Gets abuse from both sets of players for either flagging or not flagging offside. His own team think he is being disloyal, and the opposition think he's biased. The truth is, he hasn't been paying attention.

● No flags are available, so he is forced to use a spare sock to indicate a throw-in.

● Occasionally forgets that he is the linesman and has to sprint 30 yards to try to catch up with play.

● At least once a game he will collide with a spectator that is too close to the pitch (often The Angry Dad, see page 54).

Key attribute:
NOT GOOD ENOUGH TO MAKE IT INTO THE STARTING ELEVEN
Sunday League value:
9/10

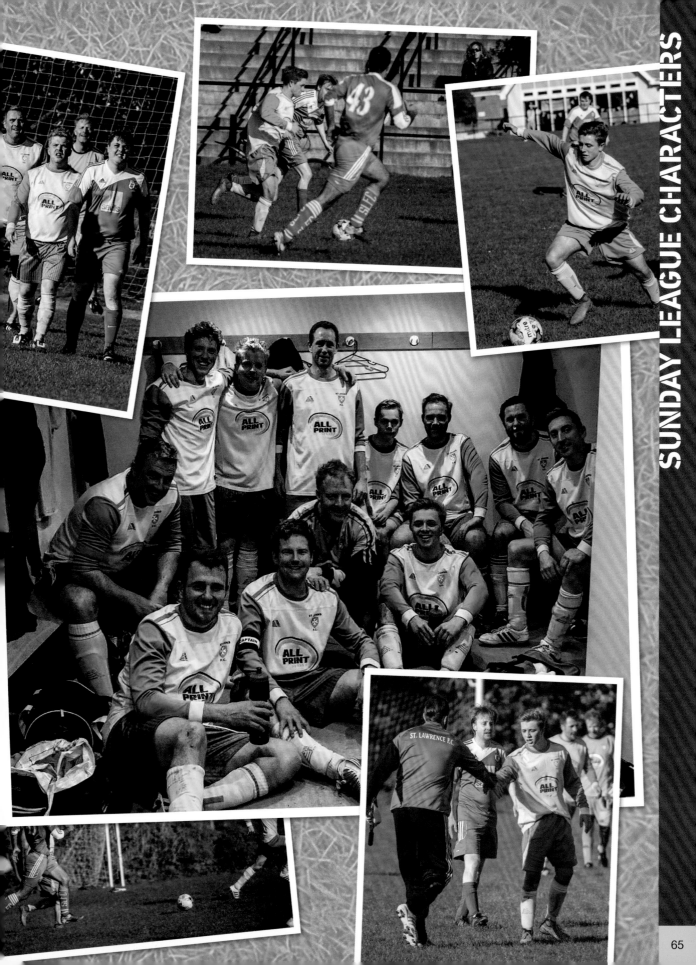

Family Album 4

My first taste of fame – on the back page of the 'Jersey Evening Post'. No autographs, please.

Ollie and me, playing on the original Xbox. I've given him the unfeasibly big controller for the extra advantage. It's my Xbox, Ollie. Fight me.

He can't even reach all the buttons! You're a horrible cousin. (Also, did you just switch between different football kits for your entire childhood?)

First ever real
football match
in Year 4, at
the Fortress.

Come on, Ollie. You
could have held it in
until we got home.

You are disgusting.

First trophy under
the belt! Won with
'Mini-Madrid' in a
tournament in Jersey.

*I always assumed you
just got those for
taking part.*

CHRIS'S TOP FIVE INSPIRATIONAL FOOTBALLERS

5. CESC FABREGAS

My childhood hero. He was the Arsenal player I always tried to base my game on, because I was quite small when I was younger so it was all about passing. I'm not quite sure what happened to him after 2011 when he left us (he just disappeared off the face of the planet, I guess). I've not followed his career since then. Hope he's doing well.

My Top 3 Fabregas memories:

1. His 30-yard screamer against Tottenham when we beat them 3-1 in 2007.

2. The solo goal he scored against Spurs in 2009 when he dribbled from the halfway line.

3. A free-kick he scored against Aston Villa in 2009. We really needed the win at the time and he came off the bench to score a beauty.

Best attribute: Passing/vision

Fabregas shirts in my collection: 3
(Not sure where they are these days, though. They seem to have gone missing from my wardrobe for some reason.)

Best season: Probably 2010/11, when Arsenal almost won the league, before Eduardo broke his leg. It feels like a long time ago!

Idol rating: 6

It would be higher if he hadn't disappeared. Oh well. I guess some things are better left as mysteries.

4. THIERRY HENRY

This man needs no introduction. Undoubtedly Arsenal's greatest ever striker and the player even non-Arsenal fans looked up to. His name was the first I ever had on the back of a shirt. He had it all – dribbling, pace, finishing – and was a joy to watch. He was so inspirational that I would say he revolutionized the Premier League. And he always scored against Spurs, which helped.

My Top 3
Henry memories:

1. The goal in the FA Cup against Leeds on his second debut in 2012. He'd re-joined Arsenal on loan from New York Red Bulls, and he scored just nine minutes after coming on as a sub. It's possibly the closest I've been to crying at a goal. Is that sad? Judge me.

2. His goal against Real Madrid in the Champions League in 2006 when he went past four players and slotted it in the bottom right. That was the season we almost won the Champions League (which also feels like a long time ago).

3. The goal against Manchester United in 2000 when he flicked it up and volleyed it into the top corner.

Best attribute: His trademark open-foot finish

Henry shirts in my collection: 3

Best season: The year he was part of 'The Invincibles', when Arsenal won the league without losing a game in 2003/04. He was the league's top scorer.

Idol rating: 10

3. ROBERT PIRES

He won Player of the Season in his first year at Arsenal, despite being injured for a large part of it. I think that speaks for itself! He was never quite the same after that injury but he was still Robert Pires. Attacking, direct and good on the ball, he was always an exciting player to watch.

My Top 3 Pires memories:

1. He scored an amazing goal against Liverpool during 'The Invincibles' season, a curling shot into the top right at Anfield.

2. One of his best goals was against Spurs in that incredible 5-4 game at White Hart Lane in 2004. I spent years as a kid trying to do that shimmy, where he moved the ball from one foot to another. I didn't get the chance to try it against him at Wembley, unfortunately.

3. It has to be me flicking the ball over his head during the Wembley Cup. (Not that I mention it much!)

Best attribute: Dribbling

Pires shirts in my collection: 1

Best season: He racked up loads of goals and assists during 'The Invincibles' season in 2003/04.

Idol rating: 9

THIS HAPPENED, RIGHT?

2. DAVID BECKHAM

The two teams I follow are Arsenal and England and, when I was younger, 'Becks' was the English version of Thierry Henry. He was THE player to look up to in the England team, but I probably don't have to tell you that. I'd love to do a free-kick challenge with Beckham one day – that would be crazy. I don't think I'd have much chance of winning, though. Editing doesn't work if he's standing next to you in real life. He'll still be brilliant at free-kicks ten years from now.

My Top 3 Beckham memories:

1. That last-minute free-kick against Greece which meant England qualified for the 2002 World Cup.

2. His penalty against Argentina in that World Cup was a huge moment as well. There was so much pressure on him and he nailed the celebration too.

3. I was only two months old when he scored from the halfway line for Manchester United in 1996 but I must have watched it on YouTube dozens of times.

Best attribute: Free-kicks
Beckham shirts in my collection: 2
Best season: It has to be 2002. He carried the England team that year.

Idol rating: 9

1. THE FATHER

Sigh He didn't even pressure me into this one. For years I used to be there on the sideline of his games, half-watching him play, half-messing around with a ball. He would always play either up front or as an attacking winger. My dad was really fast back then and very good at dribbling – a bit like a mix of Henry and Pires. He'll love that. Unfortunately, by the time I was old enough to play in the same team most of his pace had drained away (as I love to remind him in games now!). He's still going strong at 51 though, so I suppose I can cut him a little slack.

My Top 3 Dad memories:

1. He scored three consecutive hat-tricks playing for St Lawrence, a team in Jersey. It used to get mentioned at least once a week when I was younger!

2. The first assist I gave him when we were playing together. I turned a defender and put it on a plate for him.

3. Him refereeing my first football birthday party! It was England vs England. The only frustrating thing was he didn't give me ANYTHING in the way of decisions. I think you have to slightly overcompensate if your son's on the pitch. A penalty or two wouldn't have gone amiss though . . .

Best attribute: Dribbling (he's always been a messy eater)

Dad shirts in my collection: 0

Best season: 1998 – the year he scored those three consecutive hat-tricks (not that he ever mentions it).

Idol rating: Ranges between -4 and 10, depending on how much he passed to me in our most recent game.

WHAT WOULD I BE . . .
IF I WASN'T A YOUTUBER!?

1.
Vet

GULP!

When?

Between the ages of fourteen and eighteen. Basically, it was what I was thinking about doing before my YouTube channel took off.

Why?

I actually had interviews with universities about studying to be a vet and I always said that I had a passion for looking after animals. Biology was always my favourite subject and I've always loved a good David Attenborough documentary. But funnily enough, I never really had any pets that I was especially close to (apart from Santi – see page 94).

What put you off?

Not being accepted by the universities I applied to was probably the biggest obstacle! But I also began to realize I didn't quite have the level of passion needed for it. Finding out that vets have to 'put down' a lot more animals than you think was a bit of a downer too. I didn't really want to spend my life killing people's pet cats . . .

2.
Red Arrows pilot

When?
Between the ages of six and eight.

Why?
Jersey has an air show every year and I was obsessed with it. Like, OBSESSED. I remember one year my parents wouldn't allow me to go because I'd behaved badly at school or something, and I still stand by my claim that it's the saddest I've ever been. Also, my grandad was a wing commander in the RAF, so it runs in the family.

What put you off?
Realizing that the chances of being a Red Arrows pilot were very slim. Also, I'd probably have had to go to war for a few years. You can't just start off as a Red Arrows pilot, apparently!

3.
Professional footballer

When?

From when I was born to now.

Why?

I can't even remember particularly when
or why. I think it's just something that
happens if you're raised in a football-loving
family. Beckham's free-kick against
Greece in particular (see page 72) made
me think 'I want that'. I can't even imagine
what he felt like at that moment. I used to
re-create his goal celebration whenever I
scored a screamer into the small goals in our
garden. Good times. Thinking about it, the
closest I've come to that is my goal in the
2017 Sidemen match. Not a bad effort!

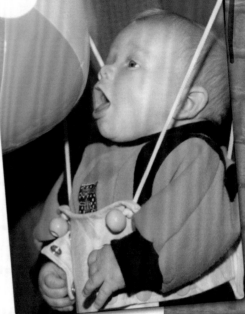

What put you off?

My height! They always picked the bigger players in junior
football, which was really frustrating. It's a bit of an English
thing. Maybe in Spain I'd have flourished and replaced Iniesta.
Thanks, Mum and Dad. Also, it's probably a tough job. I do think
that people forget that footballers are human, too. The media
are obsessed with them but they are just normal people. I'll just
wait for the phone call from Arsenal.

4. Movie director

When?

Between the ages of nine and ten. It was the most productive time of my life, when I was making the epic Nerf Wars films.

Why?

We made so many films as kids. The Nerf Wars are just the tip of the iceberg. I was always in charge – I was director, lead actor and producer! I pretty much forced everyone in my family to take part. And I still have some videos of football tournaments that Kelly and I created with our toys . . . but no one is ever seeing those.

What put you off?

The cast getting fed up and complaining when I wanted a seventeenth take of them getting a bucket of water in the face. It was bad enough dealing with Kelly and Ollie. Imagine having to work with professional actors.

5.
Palaeontologist

When?

Between the ages of five and six.

Why?

I was obsessed with the 'Jurassic Park' films and the computer game 'Jurassic Park: Operation Genesis' that went with them (some of my earliest videos about this game are still on my second channel). Also, the Natural History Museum was a frequent destination when I was younger. Since you're asking, my favourite dinosaur was the Liopleurodon, a massive predator that used to live in the sea. Much better than a T-Rex (so mainstream).

What put you off?

Finding out that it's not a very well-paid job. I would still love to do something where I was finding out about dinosaurs, but I don't think there are many bones buried in Jersey. Maybe I'll do a video about it one day.

Family Album 5

It took me a long time to catch my first fish. This was probably only hour two, as I'm still standing up.

And I'm not there. Meaning it's definitely already hour two.

Or it's hour four and you're in the water.

NOW LET'S TALK ABOUT YOUR BALL CONTROL IN THE 12TH MINUTE OF LAST WEEKEND'S GAME . . .

Fishing with my old man in the Lake District.

First fish I ever caught solely by myself. Magnificent. (My ears that is, not the fish.)

I was going to comment on the haircut, but the ears thing works too.

Sporting the Pires shirt. Was totally a dream come true to play against him. (See page 70!)

I would make fun of Ollie's shirt but looking at my jeans I'm in no place to comment.

My Top Ten Sunday League Moments

My family have been filming my Sunday League matches since I was old enough to kick a ball. Here are my favourite moments, good and bad, that really sum up Sunday League for me. Let's count them down . . .

10.

A glorious own goal
Season: 2009/10

This was a defender scoring possibly the finest own goal I have ever seen. The ball was crossed by one of our players and he inexplicably headed it past his own goalkeeper. The first time you watch this clip, it looks as if a striker has scored a bullet header. It's only the second time round that you realize he's put it in his own net.

9.

Charlie being Charlie
Season: 2014/15

My mate Charlie has always been one of those dark horses when it comes to football skills, but he lets himself down badly here. He just seems to forget that he's a footballer and hoofs the ball away. The way he shifts from Ronaldinho to Ryan Shawcross in two seconds is simply incredible.

8. Dog stops play (or not)

Season: 2015/16

Many Sunday League players will have experienced a dog running on to the pitch. What I love most about this clip is that no one stops playing – we just keep on going (while making sure the dog doesn't get too close to our ankles). The owner does nothing, of course. To be fair, the dog was marginally more effective than most of the players, but we couldn't catch him to sign him up for the rest of the season.

7. Dog commits cynical foul

Season: 2015/16

My mum knows to keep an eye out for funny action when she's filming and she was the one who spotted this (much to my delight). It's just a dog casually stopping to poo on the corner flag, right in the middle of a match. The owner is nowhere to be seen, which is probably for the best. It's not the same dog as in the above clip. It's a much bigger animal, unfortunately.

PICK IT UP!

6.

Paying the penalty for a poor pitch
Season: 2013/14

I've never seen a penalty spot in a worse state than this one. It looks like a gang of rugby players have been mud-wrestling in the rain for three days on top of it. Mostly we try to avoid it, but in this clip Jamie's shot hits a lump in the penalty spot and completely changes direction. Completely. It's like a glitch in *The Matrix*. You can't really blame the keeper for this one.

5.

One step-over too many
Season: 2015/16

This is a perfect example of the price you pay for trying too many step-overs in a Sunday League game. To be fair, everyone knows you deserve everything you get if you pull out one of these. But I do love that he complains about the foul. He'll need a lawyer for this one.

4.

'Keeper's!'
Season: 2013/14

This is quite possibly the worst piece of goalkeeping ever recorded on film. The ball is coming down from the sky and the defender makes a clever decision to nod it back. And it's actually a really good header – until the wind catches it. The rest is history.

3.

'Steve Gerrard, Gerrard. He slipped on his . . .'
Season: 2015/16

I'd never actually seen a player do this before but Jeff here is not like any other player. The ball is gently rolling out towards him with no one nearby and he just falls over. For no reason. It's like he forgets how his legs work. What makes it even better is the reaction of our right-back, whose face is a mixture of frustration, disappointment and pity. He's definitely considering a transfer in that moment.

2.

He could have had trials with Barcelona
Season: 2010/11

This is a fine piece of skill that leads to a goal. The only problem for the player is that he doesn't mean it, and the goal is scored into his own net. It wouldn't really be fair to name him (I wouldn't do that to you, Phil), and in his defence we were already losing 5-0. But if you're going to score an own goal, you might as well score one as good as this.

1. Throwing it all away

Season: 2015/16

This poor guy. It's a perfect throw-in: both feet on the floor, hands behind his head, good trajectory on the ball. The one thing he hasn't taken into account is the trees overhanging the pitch. For me, it just perfectly sums up Sunday League. We have to endure things that no professional player would put up with, but everyone just gets on with it. I mean, who has a tree growing over a football pitch? Us. That's who.

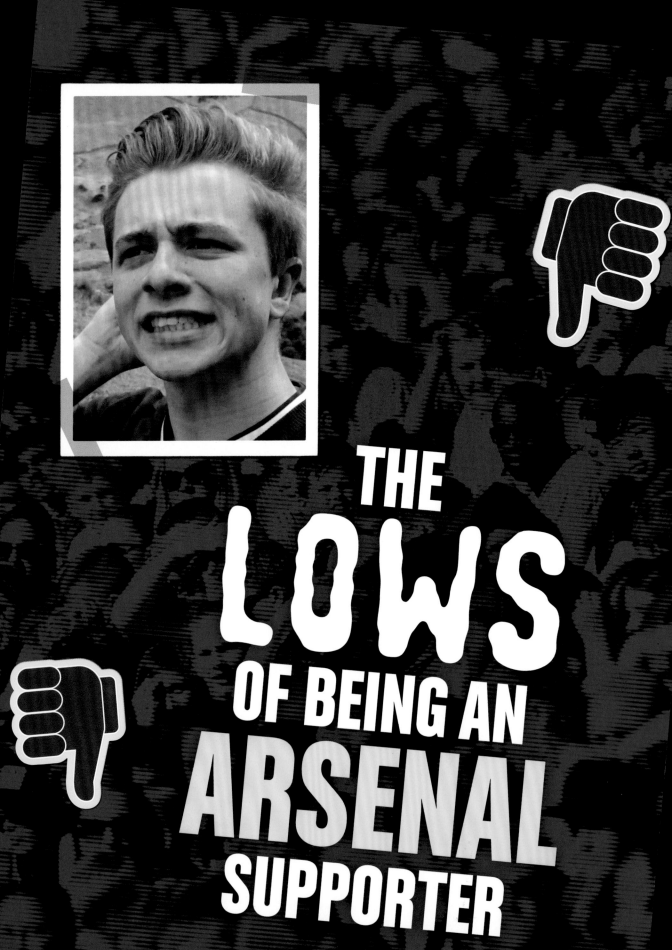

THE
LOWS
OF BEING AN
ARSENAL
SUPPORTER

Eduardo breaking his leg against Birmingham City in 2008

This was supposed to be our season. We were five points clear at the top of the Premier League going into this game and everyone felt it was only a matter of time until the title was ours. Then Eduardo broke his leg, we conceded an equalizer in the last minute and after that the whole team just seemed to fall apart. We drew the next four games and then lost to Chelsea. We eventually finished third. Which is better than fourth, I suppose. And so began the great tradition of the 'March collapse'.

Misery rating: **1/5**

Emmanuel Adebayor doing a knee slide in front of the away fans after scoring against Arsenal while playing for Manchester City in 2009

I never thought you could really hate a footballer. I mean, they're just doing their job, right? It turns out I was wrong. You could see how furious the Arsenal fans were in the crowd and we were the same at home. To be fair, I have tried replicating that knee slide but because The Fortress is never watered it usually ends up in a face plant.

Misery rating: **2/5**

Losing 8-2 to Manchester United
at Old Trafford in 2011

This was an awful game, just awful. It wasn't even a great United team – it had early Danny Welbeck, Nani, even Anderson (who even remembers Anderson?). I still watched to the bitter end, for some reason. I then stayed in my house for four days because around half of my friends at the time seemed to support Man Utd. At least we scored two goals, right?

Misery rating: **3/5**

Losing 2-1 to Birmingham City in the Carling Cup final in 2011

I don't normally meet many Birmingham fans around but I remember going to school the day after this game and there was one in my first class. Typical . . . I still see the final five minutes in nightmares. Koscielny and Szczesny hesitating, Obafemi Martins flipping in celebration. I don't really want to talk about it.

Misery rating: **4/5**

Losing the Champions League final 2-1 to Barcelona in 2006

This is one that I don't remember too well because I was so young, but what I do remember is the ref sending off Arsenal's goalkeeper Jens Lehmann. It ruined the game. I remember before the game being absolutely sure that we were going to win it. In our house we even had a lucky cuddly animal (Harry the owl) who had watched every game in the tournament. No idea where he is now. And I don't care.

Misery rating: **5/5**

THE HIGHS
OF BEING AN
ARSENAL
SUPPORTER

Finishing above Spurs in 2016/17
on the last day of the season

Spurs were ahead of us and just had to win their last game, which was against already-relegated Newcastle, to finish above us for the first time in more than twenty years. It didn't go swimmingly for them. Spurs just crumbled for absolutely no reason at all. It was their version of Arsenal's 'March collapse' and they ended up losing 5-1 to already-relegated Newcastle. Have I said that? We were all depressed at the start of the day and then Spurs did that. Thanks, Spurs. Thank you very much.

Joy rating: **1/5**

Winning the FA Cup in 2005 against Manchester United

I remember this game very well. We won it on penalties, with the winner being converted by our captain, Patrick Vieira. We were completely outplayed, and yet somehow we still managed to win it in the end. There's nothing sweeter than nicking a game that you didn't deserve, especially when it's a cup final. I always love a good penalty shoot-out, too. Who doesn't?

Joy rating: **2/5**

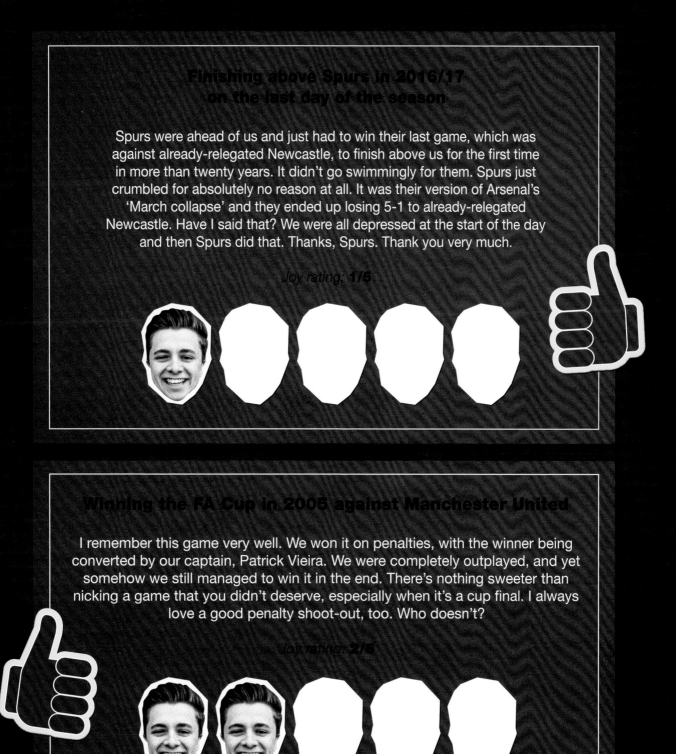

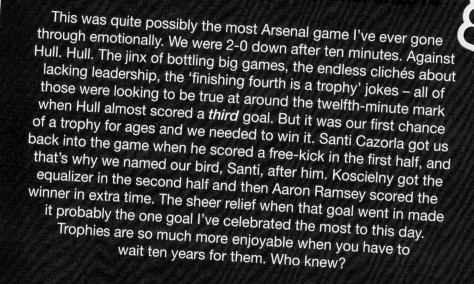

Beating Hull 3-2 in the FA Cup final in 2014

This was quite possibly the most Arsenal game I've ever gone through emotionally. We were 2-0 down after ten minutes. Against Hull. Hull. The jinx of bottling big games, the endless clichés about lacking leadership, the 'finishing fourth is a trophy' jokes – all of those were looking to be true at around the twelfth-minute mark when Hull almost scored a *third* goal. But it was our first chance of a trophy for ages and we needed to win it. Santi Cazorla got us back into the game when he scored a free-kick in the first half, and that's why we named our bird, Santi, after him. Koscielny got the equalizer in the second half and then Aaron Ramsey scored the winner in extra time. The sheer relief when that goal went in made it probably the one goal I've celebrated the most to this day. Trophies are so much more enjoyable when you have to wait ten years for them. Who knew?

Joy rating: 3/5

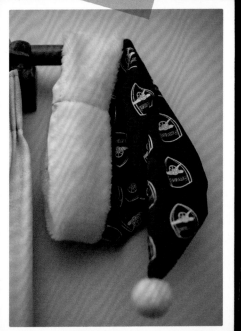

Beating Aston Villa 4-0 in the FA Cup final in 2015

This was a massive win but it was also so much more than that. The day after the game, I played in the first Wembley Cup! Just 24 hours after Arsenal thumped Aston Villa, I was walking down the same tunnel and playing football on the same grass. I even had the seat in the changing room where Alexis Sanchez had been the day before (not that I checked or anything). I reckon my goal in the Wembley Cup must have been down to that! Shout-out to Atom and Humber.

Joy rating: 4/5

'The Invincibles' season of 2003/04, when Arsenal won the Premier League without losing a game

I was spoilt with Arsenal as a kid. All I knew in my first football-conscious years were invincible seasons and FA Cup and Premier League doubles. But this is the season that really sticks in the mind. I can't imagine how the players felt. I've never had an unbeaten Sunday League season (I've had a few where we only won one or two games, though!). The team was just incredible. We had some really tough players: Martin Keown, Patrick Vieira, Ray Parlour and Thierry Henry, to name just a few. They were made of the stuff that earned them the label 'natural leaders' – that cliché the pundits love to use. We could do with a few of those these days. Natural leaders, that is – not pundits.

Joy rating: 5/5

How I Set Up for a Typical Football Challenge

1. MAIN CAMERA

This is positioned to capture the wide shot of the challenge. It's always the most important one to get right. A handy tip is to always check that it's actually switched on. There's nothing more frustrating than missing a good goal!

2. CAMERA BAG

I've also missed goals because the battery has run out, so make sure you have lots of spare batteries and memory cards in your bag. Running out of either can mean you might have to stop filming early.

3. SECOND CAMERA

If you score a good goal or do something funny, it's nice to have a second angle of it.

4. ACTION CAMERAS

I use GoPros because they are perfect for catching action shots. Oh, and it looks great when the ball hits them. Luckily, they are built to stand up to this sort of abuse. I set them up in the corner of the goal and clip them to the post.

5. iPHONE

An iPhone is very helpful for slow-motion footage, because it records at 60 frames per second. It's also useful for recording people's feet or very low shots on the move.

6. FREELANCE CAMERAMAN

Sometimes I hire an extra cameraman to walk around and capture extra footage. They sometimes manage to film things I haven't seen and it helps to put together an interesting video.

7. BALL-RETRIEVAL ASSISTANT

This is usually either someone I've hired to help out for the day, or a family member! Of course, sometimes you get fans hanging around during filming and they're happy to help out too.

8. FREE-KICK MANNEQUINS

These are a bit of a nightmare to transport to and from the pitch, because they're so big. The ones I have are all a bit broken now, having got in the way of too many wayward shots. But they do make videos look a bit more professional.

9. BALL BAG

Not having enough balls makes everything take much longer. I try to have around 30 balls available for a video (which means I have to spend quite a lot of time pumping them up beforehand). I always lose one or two – especially at The Fortress, where they get eaten up by the bushes!

10. BOUNCE RAMP

These are great for teeing up the ball for volleys. They also tend to be a bit more reliable than your mates, especially if you're playing against them in a challenge!

Family Album 6

Taking my love for 'The Gunners' a little too far.

Oh, good lord. A prime specimen of the human race.

You could land a plane on those things.

Ah, night-time fishing in the Lake District. Note how I've positioned Ollie so that he must go through me to escape back home.

His eyes look sad.

Again, no route of escape. I wasn't stupid.

There's simply no caption needed.

One Football Challenge to RuleThemAll

RuleThemAll

You've seen me doing countless football challenges, and now it's your turn!

In this challenge there are ten rounds. Each one is scored out of five, giving you a final score out of 50. Check your position on the leaderboard opposite and see how you compare to me, Ollie, Kelly and other YouTubers.

To ensure that everything is fair, all you need for each of the ten upcoming challenges is a ball and a goal.

Good luck!

Use #RuleThemAll on social media to share your videos of you doing the challenges and I'll make a compilation of your best (and worst!) efforts.*

All you need to take part is a pitch and a ball (a family member to do your filming is entirely optional, but it helps).

*Submissions from those aged 13 or under must be accompanied by evidence of permission from a parent/guardian or with their written consent.

Keeping Score

Write your scores for each challenge below and total them up. Then take a look at the YouTubers' leaderboard and see how you compare!

	YOUR SCORES
Challenge 1:	/5
Challenge 2:	/5
Challenge 3:	/5
Challenge 4:	/5
Challenge 5:	/5
Challenge 6:	/5
Challenge 7:	/5
Challenge 8:	/5
Challenge 9:	/5
Challenge 10:	/5
TOTAL SCORE:	/50

POSITION	NAME	SCORE
1	F2 (taking turns)	33/50
2	Manny	23/50
3	Theo Baker	22/50
4	Chris	20/50
4	Simon (Miniminter)	20/50
6	Toby	19/50
7	Spencer Owen	18/50
8	Harry (W2S)	17/50
9	Calfreezy	16/50
10	Callux	15/50
11	Ollie	14/50
12	Kelly	6/50

1. Crossbar Challenge from the Penalty Spot

Rules:

- You have five attempts for this challenge.
- If the penalty spot is ruined, you can place the ball to the side of it – but not any closer to the goal.
- Place the ball on the spot, take a run-up and attempt to hit the bar.
- You score one point if the ball touches the bar. (Even skimmers count.)

My top tips:

- *I don't go for power. I prefer a 'dink'. If it was golf, I'd be using a pitching wedge.*
- *If you use less power, you don't have so far to run to retrieve the ball!*
- *Don't try trick shots. It's the first challenge, so no messing around with rabonas!*

Your score:

/5

Hitting the Post from the Penalty Spot

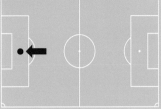

Rules:

- You get five attempts.
- Just like last time, the ball can go to the side of the penalty spot if it's ruined, but you can't move the ball closer to the goal!
- Place the ball on the penalty spot, take a run-up and attempt to hit the post.
- You score one point for striking either post (the bar doesn't count!).

My top tips:

- *Your approach depends on the quality of the pitch. If it's a good surface, I recommend calmly rolling it along the floor.*
- *If the turf has a few divots or molehills, try a delicate chip.*

Your score:

/5

3.

Keepy-Ups

Rules:

- You have five attempts for this challenge, but you only use your highest score.

- Start with the ball in your hands and see how many times you can keep it in the air.

- You can use any part of your body to keep it up (apart from your hands or arms, obviously!).

- The challenge ends when the ball touches the floor.

- You score no points for nine kicks or below, one point for reaching ten kicks, two points for 20, three points for 30, four points for 40, and five points for 50 or above.

Kicks	Points
< 9	0
10	1
20	2
30	3
40	4
50	5

My top tips:

- Concentrate on your stronger foot – there's no shame in that.

- Knees get you a lot of points, so make sure you use 'em!

- Don't move around too much. Try to stay in one place.

- Don't try this in the house. It will not end well (speaking from experience).

Your score:

/5

4.

Passing the Ball into the Six-Yard Box from the 'D'.

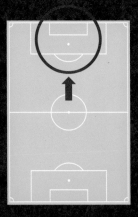

Rules:

- As usual, you get five attempts.

- Place the ball anywhere inside the 'D' on the edge of the penalty area, and hit the ball into the six-yard box.

- You score one point if the ball stops inside the area (on the line counts).

My top tips:

- *Check the wind beforehand. Inches count, so every advantage you can get will help.*

- *If this was a golf shot, you'd be reaching for the putter. No chipping here.*

- *Less is more. Try not to use too much power.*

Your score:

/5

5.

Crossbar Challenge from the Edge of the Box

Rules:

- You have five attempts.
- Place the ball anywhere on the 18-yard line (the edge of the penalty box).
- You score one point if the ball touches the bar. Again, skimmers count.

My top tips:

- *It can be easier to aim for the top corner of the goal. Pretend you're trying to score a screamer!*
- *Make sure the ball is on a nice patch of grass. Divots won't help.*
- *If you have more than one ball, you won't be running to retrieve it all the time (a willing sibling can come in very useful).*

Your score:

/5

6. Weak Foot Crossbar Challenge from the Edge of the Box

Rules:

- Five attempts!

- Place the ball anywhere on the edge of the penalty box.

- You must use your weaker foot. The outside of your stronger foot does not count!

- You score one point each time the ball touches the bar. Skimmers count!

My top tips:

- *Make sure you plant your standing foot close to the ball. That always makes a difference for me.*

- *Don't give up if your first few attempts are awful. Just give it a bit of welly and you never know!*

Your score:

/5

7.

Corner Challenge

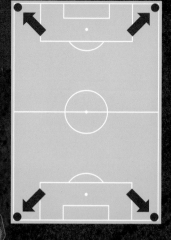

Rules:

- You know the drill by now – you get five attempts!
- This is the trickiest one so far. The aim is to curl the ball into the goal from a corner.
- The ball can be anywhere in the quadrant (just remember to remove the flag, if there's one there).
- You score one point if the ball ends up in the goal, even if it hits the post first.

My top tips:

- *Picking a windy day can help. Just make sure the wind is blowing towards the goal and not away from it!*
- *Ideally, you want the ball to bounce just before the near post. Hopefully, the spin on the ball will help take the ball into the goal.*
- *Really wrap your foot round the ball.*
- *Watch a video of any David Beckham set piece!*

Your score:

/5

8. Weak Foot Corner Challenge

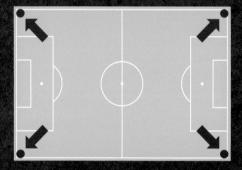

Rules:

- It's getting seriously tough now, but you still only get five attempts.
- Again, you're trying to curl the ball into the goal from a corner – but this time you have to use your weak foot.
- The ball can be anywhere in the quadrant.
- You score one point if the ball ends up in the goal. Post-and-in is fine.

My top tips:

- *I'm not going to lie – this is a difficult round. Just adopt the brace position and we'll get through it.*
- *Once again, the wind is your friend. It's worth waiting for a huge gust.*
- *It's probably best to save this challenge for when no one is watching.*

Your score:

/5

9. No-Bounce Goal from the 'D'.

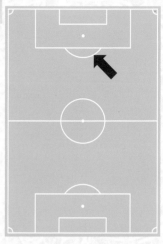

Rules:

- Five attempts!
- Place the ball anywhere on the line of the 'D' and attempt to score without the ball bouncing.
- You score one point for each successful goal. If the ball hits the post or bar on the way in, it counts!

My top tips:

- *You need to drive the ball low and hard. Knuckleballs (if you can do them) are perfect.*
- *Chipping is much more difficult, but if you're struggling you can try it.*
- *Hitting a ball straight can be hard, so you could try curling it instead.*

Your score:

/5

Scoring from the Halfway Line

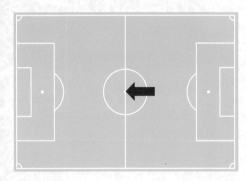

Rules:

- As usual, you get five attempts.

- Place the ball anywhere on the halfway line and attempt to kick the ball into the goal.

- You score one point for each goal you score.

- It doesn't matter if it bounces or hits the woodwork, as long as it crosses the line!

My top tips:

- *This challenge is harder than it looks. You need power and accuracy, so don't rush it.*

- *If you're struggling to reach the goal, do what every football coach says not to do – lean back! This should give you more height on the ball.*

- *Toe-pokes are allowed. But be warned – you might end up hitting the corner flag (which doesn't score you any extra points).*

Your score:

/5

Family Album 7

Look how adorable we all are. I SAID, LOOK HOW ADORABLE WE ALL ARE.

Jenny missed the football shorts memo in the squad chat.

There's always one.

You just had to be different.

No, Chris, that's not a swimming costume.

Me and my slopes, man.

**THAT.
AIR.
THOUGH.**

True or False?

**Five are true, but five are FALSE.
Can you guess which are which?**

		TRUE	FALSE
1.	I once scored against an Everton junior side.	☐	☐
2.	There's an extra Nerf Wars video that I've never uploaded because it ends with Ollie having to go to hospital.	☐	☐
3.	In my career, I've scored more free-kicks in matches than Dimitri Payet.	☐	☐
4.	A bit like Lionel Messi, I was given growth hormones when I was younger because I wasn't considered tall enough for my age.	☐	☐

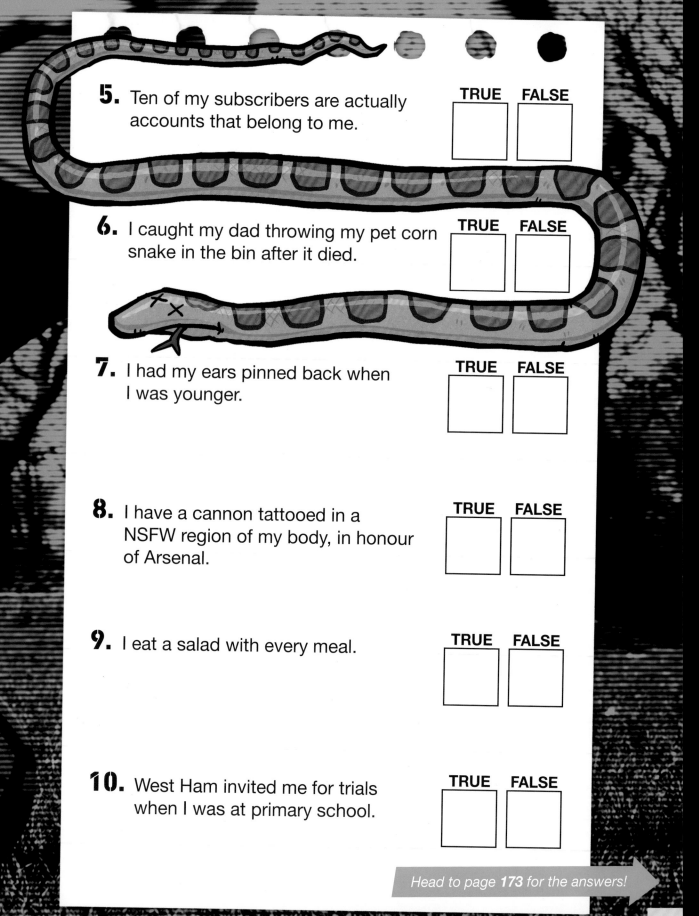

5. Ten of my subscribers are actually accounts that belong to me.

TRUE ☐ FALSE ☐

6. I caught my dad throwing my pet corn snake in the bin after it died.

TRUE ☐ FALSE ☐

7. I had my ears pinned back when I was younger.

TRUE ☐ FALSE ☐

8. I have a cannon tattooed in a NSFW region of my body, in honour of Arsenal.

TRUE ☐ FALSE ☐

9. I eat a salad with every meal.

TRUE ☐ FALSE ☐

10. West Ham invited me for trials when I was at primary school.

TRUE ☐ FALSE ☐

*Head to page **173** for the answers!*

THE EVOLUTION OF A SUNDAY LEAGUE FORMATION

STAGE 1

IN THE CHANGING ROOM, THE MANAGER EXCITEDLY ANNOUNCES THAT HE HAS SPENT THE LAST WEEK WORKING OUT A NEW FORMATION. HE DESCRIBES IT AS A 'CONTINENTAL 2-3-1-3 WITH INVERTED WINGERS'. THEN SOMEONE POINTS OUT THAT 2-3-1-3 ONLY ADDS UP TO NINE PLAYERS. HE THEN CHANGES IT TO A 4-1-2-3 AND TELLS THE TEAM THEY ARE GOING TO PLAY POSSESSION FOOTBALL LIKE BARCELONA.

STAGE 2

AFTER FIVE MINUTES OF PLAY, IT'S OBVIOUS THAT NO ONE KNOWS WHERE THEY'RE SUPPOSED TO BE PLAYING. THE CENTRE-BACK SUDDENLY FINDS HIMSELF IN THE OPPOSITION'S PENALTY AREA AND GIVES THE BALL AWAY. THE ONLY PEOPLE LEFT IN DEFENCE TO TRY TO STOP THE COUNTER-ATTACK ARE A STRIKER AND A LEFT WINGER. THE OTHER TEAM SCORES. THIS HAPPENS THREE TIMES IN THE FIRST 20 MINUTES.

STAGE 3

THE MANAGER STARTS SCREAMING THAT HE WANTS 'TWO HOLDING MIDFIELDERS' IN A DESPERATE ATTEMPT TO REORGANIZE THE TEAM. THE TEAM FINISHES THE HALF 4-0 DOWN, WITH THREE RIGHT-BACKS.

STAGE 4

IT'S BACK TO BASICS AT HALF-TIME, WITH THE MANAGER ANNOUNCING THAT THE TEAM IS SWITCHING TO A CLASSIC 4-4-2. EVERYONE IS RELIEVED, BUT WITH SO MANY ATTACKING PLAYERS ON THE PITCH IT MEANS THAT ONE OF THE STRIKERS HAS TO PLAY IN DEFENCE. THEY EMERGE FROM THE CHANGING ROOM DETERMINED TO PUT THINGS RIGHT AND TO OVERTURN THE 4-0 SCORE LINE.

STAGE 5

WITH 15 MINUTES TO GO, THE SCORE IS NOW 4-1 AND THE MANAGER CHASES THE GAME BY BRINGING ON TWO ATTACKING PLAYERS FOR TWO DEFENDERS. NOW PLAYING A FORMATION THAT LOOKS LIKE 1-2-7, THE TEAM LETS IN THREE MORE GOALS IN THE FINAL MINUTES. AFTER THE GAME, THE MANAGER PROMISES THE TEAM THAT HE WILL COME UP WITH A NEW FORMATION IN TIME FOR NEXT WEEK.

What's Behind Me?

My background has changed quite a bit over the years, but I like to keep it looking familiar. I think subscribers feel a connection when things don't change too much. I gradually add items here and there, and hopefully it will keep changing as I get to do more interesting challenges.

7

6

CHRISMD

10

1

2

14

1 100,000 subscribers plaque

This gets sent out by YouTube when you reach 100,000 subscribers. I got mine about two and a half years ago. At the time, I thought I'd made it and wouldn't get much bigger. I never expected to be where I am now. I like having it up because it reminds me of how this all started. It was a bit of a gamble putting it above my bed because it's quite heavy and I'm sure it's going to fall off and injure me eventually.

2 Medal from the first Wembley Cup

This was my winner's medal from the first charity game we played at Wembley in 2015 (no idea where the runners-up medal is from the second game!). I helped earn this medal by scoring an absolute screamer from eight yards.

3 Shirt from the first Wembley Cup

When I washed this, some of the logo wore off on the front. That's why I hung it up back to front, but now I prefer it that way! Also, it's my favourite number. When my dad was my football coach, I used to insist on a number 10 shirt even when we were playing seven-a-side.

4 ChrisMD mug

This was from a range of merchandise I brought out two years ago. Some of my friends were teasing me about it but I sold quite a few T-shirts and mugs in the first few weeks. The furthest that I had to post one was to Australia (I remember it took 21 days to get there).

5 Shirt from the first Sidemen match

I felt like I played very well in this shirt, even though I didn't score and missed a penalty. The only thing that annoys me about this shirt is that someone decided to put a space between Chris and MD. Grrr!

6 Shirt from the second Sidemen match

Probably the pride of my shirt collection. At least until I score a 90th-minute goal in front of 100,000. Number 10, red and medium size instead of baby elephant.

7 Framed picture of Atom and Humber, Alexis Sanchez's dogs

My family got me this for a Christmas present because I follow the Instagram account for Atom and Humber. I'll always stay loyal to the dogs, long after Sanchez has left the club. Dogs are for life, not just for Arsenal.

CHRISMD

8 1 million subscribers plaque

This was sent out so late by YouTube that I was already on 1.7 million subscribers by the time it arrived. It's far too heavy to put on the wall above my bed so I'm not really sure what to do with it. Now that Kelly's at university I might knock through to her room to gain some more wall space.

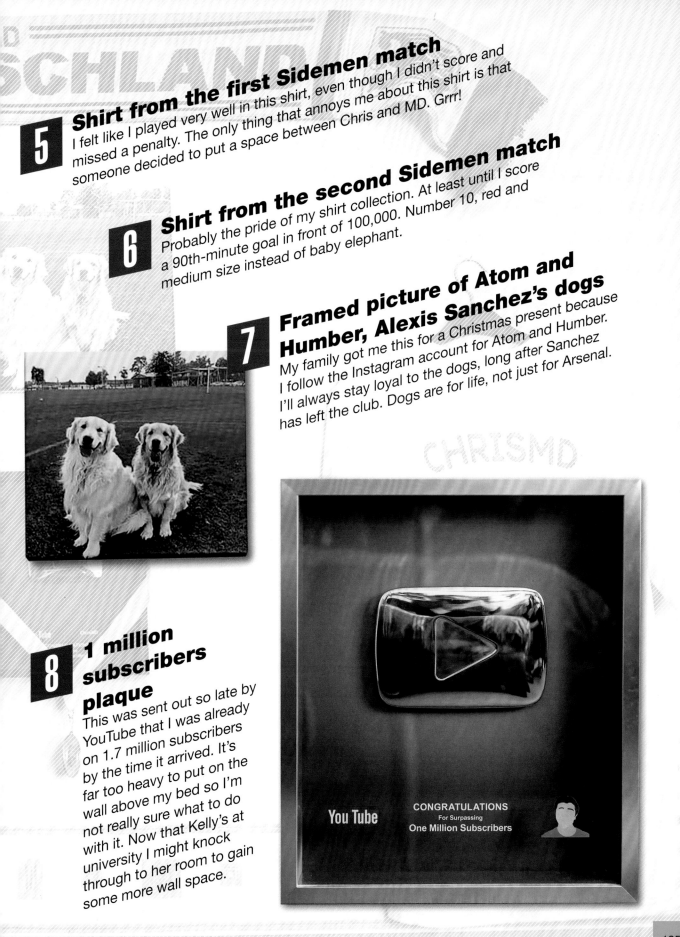

You Tube

CONGRATULATIONS
For Surpassing
One Million Subscribers

9 Arsenal bin
This is the one thing left over from my childhood bedroom. It's very old but I can't think of anything more boring than buying a new bin to replace it.

10 Tiny wardrobe
This is possibly the smallest wardrobe in the world. It's a constant battle to squeeze in smart shirts and football shirts so everything ends up on the floor.

11 'ON AIR' sign (outside the bedroom door)
I bought this light to let my family know when I was recording videos because they always used to interrupt me halfway through filming.

12 TV
This is so I can watch *Match of the Day* in bed. Priorities.

13 Guitar
I've had quite a few requests from fans to play the guitar in a video. It's time to finally give in and pick up a plectrum.

14 Bed
I upgraded from a single to a double in 2016. Genuinely life-changing. Although since the absolute monster one in Abu Dhabi, I've been left wanting more.

15 Adult bed sheets
For a few teenage months I did have a *Lord of the Rings* duvet for a while as a joke, but then I realized that some people might think I was serious, so I changed it. Some viewers might remember the old Arsenal duvet, which was in some of my early videos.

Family Album 8

How do you do, fellow kids?

You two seem to have got weddings and funerals confused pretty badly.

Picking up an award at a football tournament in Guernsey, wearing my boots signed by Matt Le Tissier. Mum still claims she doesn't remember throwing them away. Sure, Mum. Suuuuuuuuure.

You took Ollie along to record with you even then?

The commitment levels are so very real.

First trip to The Emirates! I look ready to start Arsenal Fan TV right there and then.

Ah, the football game I wasn't invited to.

5

FIFA 15: The Best Pack Opening of All Time?

Featuring: **Me!** *(And Lionel Messi and Cristiano Ronaldo)*
Uploaded: **January 2015**

What happened:

It's annoying because I've now got five or six videos titled 'Best Pack Opening Ever!' because I keep beating them. My commitment to the clickbait wasn't that strong back then. But this was the first time that I'd got Messi and Ronaldo cards on the same day, which was almost unheard-of at the time. I was streaming the pack opening to about 15,000 people and the video was a huge success.

Five Videos

Behind the scenes:

This was one of the last videos that I streamed and I've never really addressed why. The videos I record when streaming are generally a lot worse. You can't redo punch-lines or anything and, during this stream, I spent almost every minute responding to people in the live chat, which ruined my reactions to packs. Also, when people are donating hundreds of pounds at a time to support you, it feels a bit uncomfortable. I completely get that fans do it because they appreciate your work, but many other people in the world need that money more than I do!

Some people don't realize, but these pack openings can be really expensive. You might spend thousands of pounds over a few days because of all the packs you have to buy to make one of these videos.

When I got Messi right at the end, it was filmed on an awful camera because the battery on my main camera had run out. It was actually really lucky that I had the webcam as a back-up camera. Otherwise I would have missed my reaction and the whole thing would have been a complete waste of time!

4

Mother vs Son: The Ultimate Football Battle

Featuring: **Mum, Dad, Kelly and Ollie**
Uploaded: **January 2017**

What happened:

This was my first video with all of my immediate family and it included my mum's first appearance on my channel. We filmed it in the Lake District over Christmas and family members were either taking part or watching from the sidelines. My poor dad had to take the Christmas trees to the dump on Christmas Eve, which must have made him look like the world's biggest Scrooge!

Behind the scenes:

It had poured with rain the day before we filmed this, and the pitch we had hired was getting very muddy by the end of filming. A very concerned groundsman turned up to check on us and so did the club president, but they were very patient. The pitch would not have been so cut up if my dad hadn't taken so long to score.

My cousin Jenny is actually in this video, though you can't see her until the very end. She had the fun job of holding an umbrella over the camera for three hours to protect it from the wind and rain. I gave her a chance to get her own back, though. If you look closely, you can see her kicking one of the balls at me during my forfeit at the end.

We had to record my forfeit twice because everyone missed with the footballs the first time. They literally had one job. I bravely took one for the team, just to make sure we had a good ending to the video!

3 THE BEST EVER EURO GOALS RE-CREATION BATTLE VS MY DAD

Featuring: **Dad and Kelly**
Uploaded: **July 2016**

What happened:

This was my dad's proper debut on my channel. There was a mutual feeling that it was time he made an appearance, as not many YouTubers have a dad who's (almost) better than them at football! And over fifty! Good on him. We wanted to re-create some of the best goals from European Championships, but it turned out to be harder than we thought it would be. Much harder. This was during half-term and because there were so many kids at The Fortress we had to hire my secret-location pitch. It's hidden from the public eye, save for a few cows (who love to milk the abuse from the sidelines . . . anyone?).

MOO?

Behind the scenes:

We thought this video would take us a couple of hours. It took three days. Three. Days. Re-creating that Marco Van Basten volley was so, so hard. I'm a total perfectionist and know how often you can get home and be disappointed that you had to settle for a certain clip. So I really pushed it on this one. You could tell that my dad was losing his sense of humour by the end. That's partly why we decided to end the video with him hammering the ball into the back of my head!

Because Kelly had broken her finger, we had to tell her to stay away from the ball while she was in goal in case she made it worse. She was the first goalkeeper in history who was actually trying to avoid the ball.

The goalmouth was so overgrown that me and Kelly had to spend hours cutting the grass by hand (see picture). It's a glamorous life being a YouTuber!

2

THE EXTREME ARSENAL FOOTBALL CHALLENGE
| VS KSI . . . & FT. TOBI

Featuring: JJ (KSIOlajidebt) and Tobi (TBJZL)
Uploaded: July 2016

What happened:

This was the first time I'd ever recorded with JJ (KSI) and it came about through Rule'm Sports, who arranged it. The forfeit for losing was to wear an unthinkable amount of Spurs merchandise . . . and I cannot stress enough how neither of us wanted to lose this one. Going up to the desk in Sports Direct to buy the Spurs stuff was an experience, too. It's bad enough buying a rucksack, hat, football and scarf all covered in the badges of one football team, looking like you're that full-kit guy, but when that football team is Spurs? And the entire shop's staff thinks you're that Spurs fan? Not cool, man. Not cool.

Behind the scenes:

The whole thing was based around me and JJ being Arsenal fans, and I only found out at the last minute that Tobi (a Man Utd fan) was also taking part! That's why he had to go in goal.

Weirdly enough, all of the Spurs stuff that I bought for the forfeit was eventually sent to the comedian Michael McIntyre. A mutual contact told me that his son Lucas was a big fan of my channel, so it made sense. It would have been burned otherwise. Sorry, Spurs fans – I know you'd have done the same if it was Arsenal merch.

I actually said to JJ before we recorded that swearing is totally fine, but I'd just have to bleep it out for my channel. I didn't want him changing his personality just for the sake of being PG. It's part of his humour and his whole character that makes him so naturally funny. Weirdly enough, he didn't swear once. He's a very humble and normal guy away from the camera, which was as hard for me to believe as it probably is for most of you now! But he's genuinely one of the nicest guys I've met through YouTube. I'll stop brown-nosing now. He still beat me in this video, the jammy git, and he enjoyed it. A lot.

1

JERSEY VS GUERNSEY | FOOTBALL CHALLENGES ft. WROETOSHAW

Featuring: **Harry (W2S)**
Uploaded: **March 2016**

What happened:

This was the first time I'd recorded with Harry in person. There's a great rivalry between Jersey and Guernsey, but it's all tongue-in-cheek. This is my favourite video to date. I've never been more proud of uploading anything than this. It took a day to record and three solid, twelve-hour days of editing, but it's one that I can watch back and still enjoy a year later. That's when you know you did well!

Behind the scenes:

When Harry flew over to Jersey for the video he was delayed in customs for more than an hour. I'm fairly sure they thought he was smuggling drugs. No one usually gets questioned for that long. You can imagine their faces when he brings out the line 'I make YouTube videos for a living'. Pretty sure you could have heard the collective 'OKAY, MATE' without them actually saying a word.

We had to stop recording halfway through the video because two primary school football teams turned up at either side of the pitch for a match. We had to quickly pack up our cameras and get out of there! (But not before signing a few autographs and shaking some hands. We're not monsters.)

We had a Guernsey football shirt for a forfeit, the idea being that I'd have to wear it in my next three videos if I lost. Harry couldn't actually find a Guernsey shirt in the shops though, so he had to borrow one from a friend and return it. It also meant that I had to buy a Guernsey shirt online (with my own money!) to use for the punishment videos. The things I do for views.

Family Album 9

Award for 'Most Improved Player', from when the Leeds academy came over to Jersey. (If I'd understood which kind of players sometimes get given the 'Most Improved Player' award, I might not have been so happy.)

Lads, I think you're doing sailing wrong.

Insert 'Jaws' music

Climbing in the Dolomites in Italy. Yeah, we don't really do normal, relaxing holidays.

In the same way, Jersey doesn't really do normal fishing trips.

NO.1: THE CRUYFF TURN

THIS IS THE TRICK THAT I USE MORE THAN ANY OTHER. IT'S VERY HELPFUL IN TIGHT SPACES, ESPECIALLY INSIDE THE PENALTY AREA BECAUSE EVERYONE IS AFRAID OF TACKLING YOU. NAMED AFTER THE DUTCH FORWARD JOHAN CRUYFF, IT'S SIMPLE TO USE BUT HIGHLY EFFECTIVE.

HOW TO PULL IT OFF:

1. When under pressure from a defender, shape as if you're going to shoot or cross.

2. Instead of kicking the ball, knock it back between your legs with the inside of your foot in the opposite direction to which you were running.

3. Follow the ball and hopefully watch the defender sink to the floor in a fit of discombobulated confusion.

SUCCESS RATE:
100 PER CENT (NEVER FAILS!)

SKILL RATING: **4**

POSSIBLE CONSEQUENCES
FROM ANGRY DEFENDERS:
**A CYNICAL PULL ON THE
SHIRT OUTSIDE THE BOX.**

NO.2: THE MESSI DRIBBLE

THIS IS A RELATIVELY UNKNOWN ONE . . . IF YOU'VE BEEN LIVING UNDER A ROCK FOR THE LAST FEW YEARS! IT'S LIONEL'S SIGNATURE MOVE AND HE'S DONE IT AGAINST SOME SERIOUSLY GOOD PLAYERS. IT'S QUITE SIMPLE, BUT IT COMPLETELY CONFUSES DEFENDERS. HE PRETENDS TO GO ONE WAY AND THEN GOES THE OTHER, LEAVING THE DEFENDER IN A RUINED PILE ON THE FLOOR. THIS IS SO MUCH HARDER THAN IT LOOKS AND I HAVEN'T HAD THE OPPORTUNITY TO TRY IT IN A GAME YET, DESPITE PULLING IT OFF IN TRAINING TO GREAT EFFECT.

HOW TO PULL IT OFF:

1. Stand motionless, but on your toes with the ball closer to your right foot.

2. Lift your right foot and begin to feint as if you're taking the ball left. It's important this feint is quite fast and subtle.

3. Now switch the movement of your right foot to a feint to the right instead, while lifting both feet off the floor so your left foot lands further away from the ball.

4. Make the feint larger this time, so your right foot passes completely past the ball and lands to the right of it, just after your left foot lands.

5. As the defender lunges in to tackle you, knock the ball sideways across your body with the inside of your right foot.

6. Instantly hit the ball forwards with your left foot and sprint after the ball.

7. Call a taxi for the poor defender.

SUCCESS RATE:
75 PER CENT *(UNLESS YOU'RE MESSI, IN WHICH CASE IT'S 100 PER CENT, OBVIOUSLY.)*

SKILL RATING: **5**

POSSIBLE CONSEQUENCES FROM ANGRY DEFENDERS:
STUDS DOWN THE BACK OF YOUR ACHILLES.

NO.3: THE STEP-OVER

THE CLASSIC RONALDO STEP-OVER (ALTHOUGH WHICH RONALDO I'M REFERRING TO IS UP TO YOU). CRISTIANO RONALDO LOVES TO DO THIS AT ANY POINT DURING A GAME. OR AFTER A GAME. OR WHILE OUT WALKING HIS DOG. OR WHEN HE'S IN BED. HE JUST LOVES A STEP-OVER.

HOW TO PULL IT OFF:

1. While approaching a defender, cross your foot over the ball as if you're taking the ball that way, trying to force them the wrong way.

2. Repeat as many times as you dare (see possible consequences below).

3. When the defender finally falls for one of the step-overs, take the ball in the other direction.

4. Congratulations! You are now good enough to play for Real Madrid.

SUCCESS RATE:
50 PER CENT *(DEFENDERS ARE NOT REALLY SCARED OF STEP-OVERS THESE DAYS.)*

SKILL RATING: **4**

POSSIBLE CONSEQUENCES
FROM ANGRY DEFENDERS:
DEPENDS HOW MANY YOU ATTEMPT. ONE STEP-OVER MIGHT EARN YOU A STRONG SHOULDER BARGE. MORE THAN FIVE COULD MEAN BEING ON THE RECEIVING END OF A CANTONA-STYLE KUNG-FU KICK.

NO.4: THE REVERSE STEP-OVER

THIS IS VERY HANDY FOR STRIKERS, OR FOR WHEN YOU'RE PLAYING IN THE HOLE. IT WORKS VERY WELL WHEN YOU'RE SMALL AND QUICK (LIKE ME), AND YOU'RE PLAYING AGAINST A BIG, SLOW CENTRE-BACK WHO MAKES DESPERATE LUNGES FOR THE BALL.

HOW TO PULL IT OFF:

1. This is for when you receive the ball with your back to goal and a defender close behind you.

2. Lean one way and take your leg over the ball, as if you're going to dribble in that direction (left or right), but this time lead with the inside of your foot, the complete opposite of a normal step-over.

3. Next, plant your foot next to the ball and knock the ball in the opposite direction with the outside of your foot (left or right, depending on which direction you chose in the first place).

4. If the defender has bought the dummy, this should leave you with a clear path in front of you.

SUCCESS RATE:
90 PER CENT
(THIS NEARLY ALWAYS WORKS, ESPECIALLY OUT ON THE WINGS.)

SKILL RATING: **4**

POSSIBLE CONSEQUENCES FROM ANGRY DEFENDERS:
A DELAYED REACTION. EXPECT TO SUFFER A HORRIBLE TACKLE LATER IN THE GAME FROM THE SAME DEFENDER . . . WHEN HE FINALLY CATCHES UP WITH YOU.

NO.5: THE JAY-JAY OKOCHA DRIBBLE

THIS ONE IS HARD TO EXPLAIN. YOU ROLL THE BALL IN FRONT OF YOU, MAKE A DUMMY AND THEN LET IT RUN, BAMBOOZLING THE DEFENDER. OKOCHA ACTUALLY DID IT DURING THE WEMBLEY CUP WHEN I WAS IN MIDFIELD NEXT TO HIM. I CAN SEE WHY IT'S SO EFFECTIVE WHEN HE DOES IT – JUST WATCHING IT HURT MY BRAIN A BIT.

HOW TO PULL IT OFF:

1. While facing a defender, roll the ball under your studs to one side.

2. Bring the outside foot over the ball, performing a reverse step-over that sends the defender the wrong way, and allow the ball to continue rolling.

3. Follow the ball and accelerate away from the defender.

4. Look back to see the defender falling over as he tries to change direction for the third time in half a second.

SUCCESS RATE:
80 PER CENT
(ONCE YOU'VE MASTERED THIS TRICK, IT'S VERY EFFECTIVE.)

SKILL RATING: **5**

POSSIBLE CONSEQUENCES FROM ANGRY DEFENDERS:
A WILD, TWO-FOOTED SCISSOR FROM BEHIND.

Family Album 10

Well, at least it's a new Arsenal kit this time.

Sorry, did you say something? I was distracted by your haircut (or lack of).

Another day, another photo of myself attempting to brutally murder my sister.

Come and see HMS Victory, they said. It'll be fun, they said.

Profile pic material right there.

Nicely blocking me completely out of this photo except for my right foot.

Are you calling me fat?

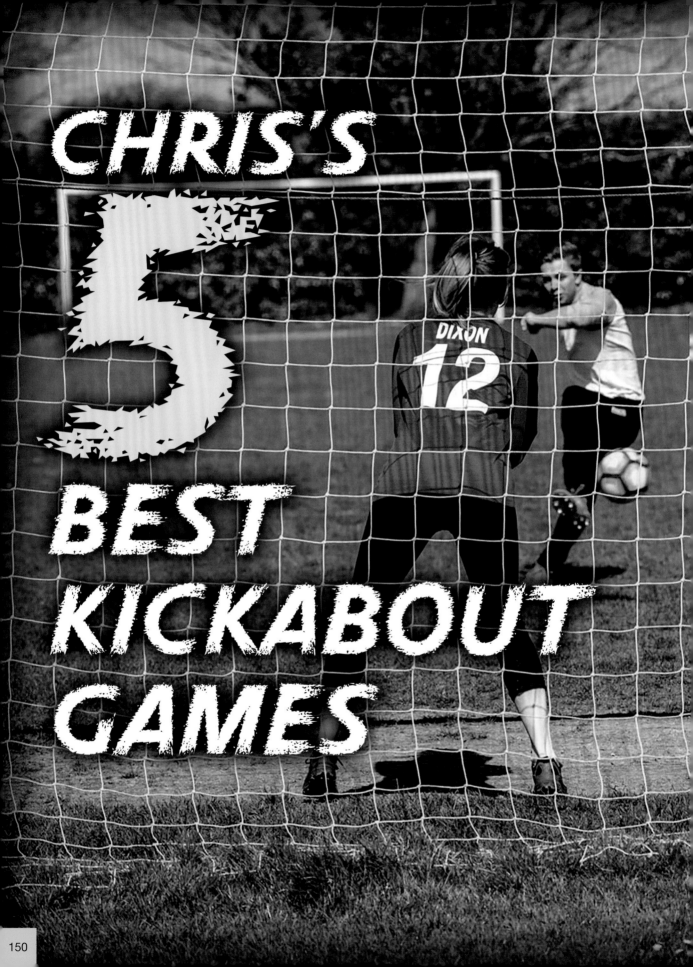

CHRIS'S 5 BEST KICKABOUT GAMES

1. WORLD CUP SINGLES

A good game to play if you only have five or six players available, or if you have an even number of players. You need a goal and a football (goalkeeper gloves are optional).

Rules:

■ Hold a penalty shoot-out to find a keeper (loser goes in goal).

■ The goalkeeper has to kick the ball out of the penalty area to start play.

■ The game is played as a tournament. You must score to progress to the next round, with one player knocked out in each round until there are two players left in the final.

■ In the final, the winner is the first player to score three goals.

Types of player involved: 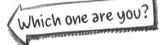 Which one are you?

■ The talented player who scores early and has to wait for ages for the round to finish because no one else can kick straight.

■ The big-boned lad who doesn't want to chase the ball but hangs around in the penalty box hoping for a rebound.

■ The super-keen dribbler who is so busy trying to beat everyone that they forget to shoot. Counts nutmegs instead of goals.

■ The annoying goalkeeper who kicks the ball as far away as possible for no reason.

■ The over-enthusiastic but usually hopeless player who is always prepared to sprint off to retrieve the ball.

■ The annoying goal-hanger who stands on the line and claims that every shot that goes in skimmed them, and therefore counts as their goal.

■ The angry player who fouls everyone because their pathetic levels of pride can't take anyone dribbling past them (often called Charlie).

■ The player who shoots from anywhere because they know it's their only chance of scoring.

WORLD CUP DOUBLES

This is the classic kickabout game that probably everyone has played at some point in their lives. The key is to always choose a good partner. Midfielders are the best players to be paired with because they want to pass the ball. Avoid full-backs at all costs.

Rules:

■ Played as a tournament, similar to World Cup Singles but with everyone in pairs.

■ Hold a penalty shoot-out to find a keeper (loser goes in goal).

■ If there is an uneven number of outfield players, the best footballer has to play by themselves.

■ The goalkeeper has to kick the ball out of the penalty area to start play.

■ Both players on each team have to touch the ball before a goal can be scored. Solo goals don't count.

■ In the final, pairs must score three goals to win.

Types of player involved:

Which one are you?

■ The lazy player who lets their partner do all the running, but still takes credit if they progress to the next round.

■ The pair of central midfielders who pass and move their way to victory like a mini Barcelona.

■ The greedy strikers who hang around in the goalmouth waiting to steal a cross that was intended for someone else.

■ The angry pair who fall out with each other because one of them won't pass to the other.

■ The goalkeeper who deliberately throws the ball to one of their mates to let them score an easy goal.

3. PIG *(Sometimes known as One-Bounce)*

This game is great if you have a ball but no goals. It's also very useful for places with no walls, such as the beach or a park.

Rules:

■ Players stand in a circle and have to keep the ball in the air.

■ You are allowed one bounce between each kick.

■ The person nearest the ball must attempt to keep it in the air.

■ Every player has three lives, and every time you lose one you spell out a letter of the word 'Pig'.

■ You lose a life if you fail to keep the ball up, or if you make it too hard for the next person to keep the ball in the air.

■ The first person to lose all their lives must face 'Red Ass'. (They have to bend over while everyone else takes it in turns to shoot at them.)

Which one are you?

OOF!

- The player who makes hospital passes which are just good enough not to be called out as cheating.

- The centre-back who always heads the ball, even if it's just a foot off the ground.

- The skilful player who never loses a life and never misses at 'Red Ass'.

- The awful player who loses all three lives in the first 30 seconds but still wants to play in each game.

- The annoying player who receives the ball more than anyone else because everyone wants them to lose.

4. SPOT

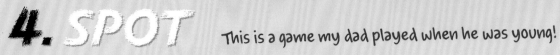

This is a game my dad played when he was young!

This is a handy game to play when you don't have an actual goal. You will need a large wall or target, though.

Rules:

■ Identify a target or area of a wall.

■ Players take it in turns to hit the ball at the target.

■ There is an agreed order of players, and everyone gets just one kick.

■ They can kick it whenever they like, whether the ball is moving or not.

■ Everyone starts with five lives and loses a life for each failed attempt to hit the target.

■ Dad and his friends were too nice to play Red Ass when they were young, so instead of doing that you finish each game with a round of gentlemanly handshakes!

Types of player involved:

Which one are you?

■ The player who gives the person following them an easy shot, so that they can then easily stitch up the next player.

■ The player who has a cannon of a shot that sends the ball miles from the target.

■ The lucky player who always sees the ball take a strange ricochet or bounce, setting it up perfectly for their turn.

■ The consistent player who always manages to hit the target, wherever the ball ends up.

5. HEADERS AND VOLLEYS

The rules to this game are more complicated than a Master's degree in astrophysics and everyone plays a slightly different version. Make sure you agree the rules before you start!

Rules:

■ The aim is to score with headers and volleys, with each goal taking lives off whoever is in goal.

■ Everyone has ten lives. The first player to lose all ten has to face Red Ass.

■ Pick a goalkeeper by having a penalty shoot-out. The loser goes in goal.

■ Goalkeepers lose one point for conceding a volley from inside the penalty area, two points for a header from anywhere, two points for a volley from outside the box, and three points for overhead kicks from anywhere.

■ If a player misses the goal or accidentally scores a goal that is not a volley or a header, they have to go in goal.

■ If the goalkeeper catches a shot, header or cross, the person who kicked the ball replaces them in goal. The goalkeeper can also throw the ball out before they leave the goal, potentially resulting in a quick goal against the player who is replacing them between the sticks.

■ While the goalkeeper is retrieving the ball from behind the goal, the others are allowed to restart play with a second ball, meaning they can score in an empty net if they are quick enough.

■ 'Post saves all!' If the ball hits the post and goes wide, it does not count as a miss.

■ 'Doggy life!' For some reason, the first person out receives a last-chance extra life.

■ 'Team goal!' If every outfield player helps keep the ball in the air before a goal is scored, the goalkeeper loses five lives.

Types of player involved:

Which one are you?

SLAP!

OW!

■ The abomination of a human being who ensures every shot they take bounces straight away to avoid any chance of having to go in goal.

■ The David Beckham fan who can't resist putting in crosses that the goalkeeper always ends up catching.

■ The poor player who attempts screamers all day but always ends up putting them over the bar.

■ The one with the thunderous right foot who is set up by everyone who doesn't like the goalkeeper.

■ That one guy who claims their set-up is never 'right to hit' and after half an hour you collectively realize is yet to make an attempt at goal.

CHRIS'S TECH SET-UP

1. Canon EOS 80D DSLR

I bought this camera because it films 60 frames per second, which is better than a lot of other options on the market. It means that I can slow down footage of me doing an overhead kick and it still looks really smooth. It's obviously quite sturdy as it's survived hitting the turf at The Fortress a few times.

I've always had Canon cameras . . . maybe because Arsenal have a cannon on their badge!

2. RØDE VideoMic Pro

This microphone is used for all my outside filming. I usually use it with a fluffy 'dead cat' cover so that it doesn't pick up the sound of the wind. Strong winds can ruin a video if you haven't protected the mic properly. Don't worry, no cats were harmed in the making of this book.

3. Sony Cyber-shot WX500

This is my second camera, which I usually put a bit closer to the action. It's a great piece of kit because it's small enough to fit in your pocket.

4. RPGT Mini Studio Continuous Lighting Kit

These lights brighten up my room, making it (and me, of course!) look better on camera. I point them at the wall and they spread the light out better than when they're aimed directly at my face. They make such a difference. If you watch some of my very old videos, they are much darker. The only downside is that the lights get quite warm, which can make it a bit uncomfortable if I'm filming a long pack-opening video in the middle of summer.

TESTING TESTING 1... 2... 3...

5. Three Samsung 24-inch monitors

I've always had Samsung monitors. These three are all linked up so that I can use the same mouse for all of them. Having three screens is very helpful for editing – it really does save time. I did consider getting four but that might get a bit complicated!

6. Blue Yeti microphone

This is only used indoors. I've been using it for three years but I'm still happy with it. The sound quality is great. I have it set up so that it doesn't pick up surround sound – just my voice.

7. Sony Vegas Pro editing software

I've used this for about six years and I've always found it to be very good. It takes so long to learn how to use an editing suite that there's not much point in changing to a different type now. Editing is a lot more complicated than many people realize, especially when you have lots of multiple 'tracks' for video, music, graphics and sound effects.

8. Xbox One and custom-made PC

I've always preferred Xbox (though I did switch to the dark side for a few months in 2015) and it's what most of my friends play. I had the computer built a few years ago and it's designed specifically for video editing. It's so much faster than my old one – it saves me hours.

9. A 4TB portable hard drive

I always have a back-up hard drive, which pretty much has my whole life on it. I even carry it on planes in my hand luggage because I'm so scared of losing it.

10. My desk

I bought this second-hand a few years ago when we redesigned my room. It's perfect for three screens because it's a corner desk and it fits neatly in the room.

11. Elgato Game Capture

This is a box that records directly from the Xbox. It's really helpful for saving all of the amazing goals you score on *FIFA* and the 5-0 drubbings you dish out to yet another gamer who is playing as Barcelona. (There are other teams, you know.)

12. Tripods

These are essential for filming and I always have a spare, just in case I break one with a wild free-kick!

Classic Sunday League Quotes

THE PITCH

Here's my handy guide to some of the stuff you're guaranteed to hear being yelled from one player to another at a Sunday League match.

'All day, lads. All day.'

This is often shouted by a defender after an opponent hits a shot from distance that sails way over the bar. It is designed to undermine their confidence and imply they can shoot from there as many times as they want. It looks a bit silly, however, when the next shot rockets into the top corner.

'Box them in!'

This is usually shouted by a centre-back, regardless of where the opposition has the ball. A far cry from Jurgen Klopp's famous gegenpressing (based around winning the ball back and launching a counter-attack) and nowhere near as effective. Unfortunately, it's usually let down by one lazy player who forgets to join in (normally the guy who shouted it in the first place).

'Get rid!'

This expression is often aimed at defenders who think they are better on the ball than they are. 'Get rid!' is at the heart of the British game and can be heard on every football pitch across the land, including Premier League grounds. It usually precedes a disastrously unsuccessful dribble that leads to a goal for the opposition. On rare occasions it's shouted with such vigour that it distracts the player about to clear the ball, leading to an air-shot and, once again, a goal for the opposition.

'How long, ref?'

The particularly unfit players start asking this around ten minutes after half-time, hoping that the game and their risk of impending cardiac arrest are nearly over.

'How many, ref?'

This will be said to the referee after an opposition player has got away with several reckless challenges without earning a booking. (Probably because the poor ref forgot his cards and is planning to finish the game 20 minutes early because it's raining.)

'I got the ball!'

Shouted by a midfielder who has just committed an awful tackle. He thinks he is innocent, however, because despite taking out two players, a spectator and the corner flag, his studs got a faint touch of the ball.

'I'll take the post!'

This is the job everyone wants at a corner. It's much easier to mark a goal post than a bruising centre-forward.

'It's still 0-0!'

A real classic. This is always shouted after your team have gone 1-0 up and is supposed to encourage everyone to keep up the same effort. It only really works if your team can't count or have very short memories.

'It's too quiet!'

Managers can be heard shouting this at their players when they have stopped 'talking' on the pitch. (Usually because for half of them it's their first game for the club and no one knows anyone else's name.)

'Never!'

An angry shout aimed at the volunteer linesman, who has just flagged up a very obvious offside. (See The Volunteer Linesman, page 64.)

'Man on!'

The opposite of shouting 'Time!'. This can be used to scare your teammates into passing you the ball. Ever gone 15 minutes without touching the ball? Not any more.

'One of you!'

This is usually shouted in frustration after two teammates run into each other while both going for the same ball.

'Ref!'

While most people will shout this at least once or twice, there is usually a red-faced centre-back on every team who spends the whole game screaming it every time a tackle, decision or pass is made (even if it's in his favour).

'Seconds!'

Always shouted in anger when someone fails to contest the second header from a goal kick. Don't be that guy. Or, if you have to be, fake a pulled hamstring and retain some dignity.

'Someone get the big man!'

Another expression heard before a corner, this is usually shouted by the guy who's just taken the post (see 'I'll take the post!', above). It's normally made in reference to the gigantic centre-back who is slowly making his way up the pitch. An alternative option is 'Big on big!', reminding everyone to mark players of similar size. This is often shouted by the smaller defenders, who are tired of marking people three times their height.

'Switch it!'

Shouted repeatedly by the worst winger in the team, even if he is marked by three players. He usually hasn't realized that everyone prefers to use the other side of the pitch because it's as far away from him as possible.

'They don't want it!'

Usually shouted just after the opposition have given the ball away and you're trying to make them feel worried. They usually respond by showing that they actually do 'want it' by scoring another goal.

'Time!'

This is supposed to tell the player in possession that none of the opposition are close by. Depending on the player's ability, this can be shouted when the opponent is either right next to them, or 50 yards away.

'Where was the shout?'

Often said by a winger who has gone on a mazy dribble and eventually lost the ball, despite ignoring clear, repeated requests from his teammates to pass to them.

Classic Sunday League Quotes

THE CHANGING ROOM

Only the lucky few (i.e. those who have turned up and remembered their kit) get to hear these expressions, reserved solely for the dressing room.

'Any injuries?'

All players ignore this question at half-time, because everyone knows what a half-time substitute means: running the line. Even if a player has a concussion and three snapped metatarsals, he will shake his head when the manager asks this.

'Don't have a go at the ref.'

Every manager says this to his players, knowing that it will be completely ignored as soon as a bad tackle is made, at which point he'll be the one leading the onslaught of personal abuse aimed at the volunteer linesman.

'He's not a real keeper so let's test him with some shots.'

The manager will issue this advice if he suspects that the opposition's goalkeeper is actually an outfield player. Which means that this advice is issued before every game of the season. Of course, the keeper usually turns out to be Manuel Neuer's cousin and keeps a clean sheet with ease.

'Hit the number nine hard in the first five and he won't want to know for the rest of the game.'

This advice normally results in a red card and a penalty – which is then scored by the number nine.

'I've got some very good players on the bench who are going to get on today.'

Managers are obliged to say this, even if the three substitutes are the worst footballers this country has ever had the misfortune of producing.

'Keep it tight for the first ten minutes.'

This tactic is usually ignored by half the midfielders and results in the team being 2-0 down to counter-attack goals after five minutes.

'Let them know you're there.'

Though this is meant to encourage the team to be physical, it is also very helpful if the opposition have forgotten that there is another team on the pitch.

'Try to win the second half.'

If their team is 7-0 down at half-time, a manager will say this in the hope that the players will salvage some pride by 'winning' the second 45 minutes. It never happens.

'Who's got tape?'

The same player always has sock tape, which is quickly used up by everyone else. This poor guy ends up spending around £367 a year making sure no one's socks fall down.

Answers to Page 118

1. TRUE. I played and scored against a junior Everton side when I was younger. I was a bit disappointed not to play against a junior Arsenal side, however, who were also in the tournament!

2. FALSE. Ollie has never been hurt in any of the Nerf Wars. The only thing that has suffered is his reputation.

3. FALSE. Despite scoring hundreds of free-kicks in my videos, including some amazing goals, I've never scored directly from a free-kick in a real game.

4. FALSE. Despite being one of the shortest in my class, I wasn't given growth hormones. Instead, I just waited for a growth spurt, which eventually raised me to the (enormous!) height I am today.

5. TRUE. (But it was a long time ago.)

6. TRUE. In my dad's defence, too many pets had already been buried in the garden . . .

7. TRUE. In Year 7, I had a procedure to have my ears pinned back.

8. FALSE. I don't really like tattoos, though I do like cannons . . .

9. TRUE. It is a running joke in the family that I always have to have a side salad. (Even if my main course is also a salad!)

10. FALSE. Even if I was asked, I'd have to say no. I could never leave The Fortress.

THANKS

There are so many people I need to thank for making this book a reality, I don't know where to start! Here goes . . .

Firstly, thanks to my co-writer, Ramsay Cudlipp, for all the hours spent at our kitchen table, reminiscing and drinking tea (even though he wanted coffee), and for his many contributions to the Sunday League sections of the book. I might even forgive him his White Hart Lane allegiance.

Thank you to Gary and the team at Puffin for their patience and for guiding me through the process of writing this book – it goes without saying that I couldn't have done this without them.

Cheers also to Liam Chivers and everyone at OP Talent for all their vital help along the way.

Big thanks to my extended family, and to my friends back home who have (nearly) always supported my decision to give the whole YouTube thing a go.

A big shout-out also to all my YouTuber mates who are always prepared to join me in videos to get me more views – you know who you are.

Thanks to Mum, Dad and Kelly for providing me with the necessary cups of tea I need to get me through the hours spent editing videos, and for their endless support in so many ways.

Finally, a massive thank-you to all my viewers for giving me the opportunity to live my dream job. You make it all possible.